Carleton Renaiss:

General Editors: Donald Beecher, Massimo Ciavolella

Carleton Renaissance Plays in Translation offers the student, scholar, and general reader a selection of sixteenth-century masterpieces in modern English translation, most of them for the first time. The texts have been chosen for their intrinsic merits and for their importance in the history of the development of the theatre. Each volume contains a critical and interpretive introduction intended to increase the enjoyment and understanding of the text. Reading notes illuminate particular references, allusions, and topical details. The comedies chosen as the first texts have fast-moving plots filled with intrigues. The characters, though cast in the stock patterns of the genre, are witty and amusing portraits reflecting Renaissance social customs and pretensions. Not only are these plays among the most celebrated of their own epoch, but they directly influenced the development of the comic opera and theatre throughout Europe in subsequent centuries.

In print:

Odet de Turnèbe, *Satisfaction All Around (Les Contens)*
Translated with an Introduction and Notes by Donald Beecher

Annibal Caro, *The Scruffy Scoundrels (Gli Straccioni)*
Translated with an Introduction and Notes by Massimo Ciavolella
and Donald Beecher

Giovan Maria Cecchi, *The Owl (L'Assiuolo)*
Translated with an Introduction and Notes by Konrad Eisenbichler

Jean de La Taille, *The Rivals (Les Corrivaus)*
Translated with an Introduction and Notes by H.P. Clive

Alessandro Piccolomini, *Alessandro (L'Alessandro)*
Translated with an Introduction and Notes by Rita Belladonna

Gian Lorenzo Bernini, *The Impressario (Untitled)*
Translated with an Introduction and Notes by Donald Beecher and
Massimo Ciavolella

Jacques Grévin, *Taken by Surprise (Les Esbahis)*
Translated with an Introduction and Notes by Leanore Lieblein and
Russell McGillivray

Lope de Vega, *The Duchess of Amalfi's Steward (El mayordomo de la
duquesa de Amalfi)*
Translated with an Introduction and Notes by Cynthia Rodriguez-Badendyck

Comparative Critical Approaches to Rennaisance Comedy
Edited by Donald Beecher and Massimo Ciavolella

Pietro Aretino, *The Marescalco (Il Marescalco)*
Translated with an Introduction and Notes by Leonard G. Sbrocchi and
J. Douglas Campbell

Lope de Rueda, *The Interludes*
Translated with an Introduction and Notes by Randall W. Listerman

Girolamo Bargagli, *The Female Pilgrim (La Pellegrina)*
Translated with an Introduction and Notes by Bruno Ferraro

Leone de' Sommi, *A Comedy of Betrothal (Tsahoth B'dihutha
D'Kiddushin)*
Translated with an Introduction and Notes by Alfred S. Golding in
consultation with Reuben Ahroni

In preparation:

About the Harrowing of Hell: A Seventeenth-Century Ukrainian Play
Translated with an Introduction and Notes by Irena R. Makaryk

A COMEDY OF BETROTHAL

"Comedy of Bethrothal"
Scene de Samson
Benedette Utili

Carleton Renaissance Plays in Translation

Leone de' Sommi, Ebreo

A Comedy of Betrothal
(Tsahoth B'dihutha D'Kiddushin)

Translated, with an Introduction and Notes, by

Alfred S. Golding

Dovehouse Editions Canada

1988

The text of *A Comedy of Betrothal* was reconstructed by J. (Chaim) Schirmann, The Hebrew University of Jerusalem, and is here translated into English by Alfred S. Golding, Theatre Department, Ohio State University, in consultation with Reuben Ahroni, Judaic and Near Eastern Languages Department, Ohio State University.

Canadian Cataloguing in Publication Data

Sommi, Leone de', 1527–1592.
    A comedy of betrothal: Tsahoth B'dihutha D'Kiddushin

(Carleton Renaissance plays in translation; 13)
Translation of: Tsahoth B'dihutha D'Kiddushin.
Includes bibliographical references.
ISBN 0–919473–79–2

I. Schirmann, Jefim, 1904–   . II. Golding, Alfred S.
(Alfred Siemon), 1924–   . III. Ahroni, Reuben. IV. Title.
V. Title: Tsahoth B'dihutha D'Kiddushin. VI. Series.

PQ4634.S53T8313 1988   852'.5   C88-090047–4

Printed in Canada

For information about the series write to:
    The Editors, Carleton Renaissance Plays in Translation
    Dept. of English
    Carleton University
    Ottawa, Ontario, K1S 5B6

For information on distribution and for all orders write to:
    Dovehouse Editions Canada
    32 Glen Ave.
    Ottawa, Canada
    K1S 2Z7

To the memory of my father, William Goldfinger (Eliezer ben Yehudah) and of my mother-in-law, Esther Auerbach (Esther bat Ya'akov)

"The memory of the righteous is a blessing."

ACKNOWLEDGEMENTS

We wish to thank the Italian Embassy in Ottawa for their support and encouragement in the publication of this volume.

PREFACE

Some years ago while doing research on Renaissance acting methodology in the *Quattro Dialoghi in Materia di Rappresentazione Sceniche* of Leone de' Sommi, Ebreo I came across the text of the same author's Hebrew language play, *Tsahoth B'dihutha D'Kiddushin*, as edited by J. Hayyim Schirmann and published by D'vir of Tel Aviv. The comedy's juxtaposition of Renaissance Italian and biblical Jewish form and content fascinated me, and I earmarked the work for later study. In 1985, while occupying the Forchheimer Chair at the Hebrew University in Jerusalem, I found the opportunity to initiate the translation of the play into English and the investigation of the background of its author. The English title, *A Comedy of Betrothal*, I took from Schirmann's own translation of the Hebrew title, found on the *verso* side of the title page in the 1965 edition, as being a most apt and clear rendering of the circumlocutory and cloudy Hebrew original. I found the play's dialogue at once fulsomely figurative and structured in parallelisms after the manner of the Hebrew Bible; yet it was also colloquial, ripe with hyperbole and often impudently direct—seeming to echo the quotidian (even street) Italian of Mantua. Similarly I recognized that Leone conceived his characters in psychological terms, while making them conform to the typology of the Italian *commedia*. They were, in fact, both lifelike and emblematic figures. I have sought, therefore, to make my translation reflect these near-contradictions, choosing to use a straightforward prose that also holds as closely as possible to the literal Hebrew while eschewing the resonances of Biblical metaphor (as this is conveyed to us through the King James English version), unless the idiom is now part of informal English.

Although the text can be enjoyed in and of itself, some knowledge of its origins, authorship and conventions can contribute to the reader's appreciation. I have therefore supplied information on Leone and his relationship to the Mantuan Jewish community and the Ducal Theatre of that city. Of special scholarly interest is my inclusion in this same introductory material of a description of the manner of mid-sixteenth-century Italian acting, and a hypothetical reconstruction of the first performance of the play, *circa* 1550.

My rendering into English of the highly idiomatic Bible- and Talmud-based Hebrew would not have been as accurate and felicitous had I not been able to consult with my friend and colleague, Dr. Reuben Ahroni, Associate Professor in the Department of Judiac and Near Eastern Languages and Literatures at the Ohio State University, and Editor of its *Hebrew Annual Review*. From his encyclopedic knowledge of the Bible and Talmud, and his own research into medieval Jewish poetry, Professor Ahroni has contributed a substantive analysis of Leone's poetic style as part of the Introduction. I am also much indebted to Rabbi Dr. Richard Sarason, Associate Professor of Rabbinic Literature and Thought, the Hebrew Union College, Jewish Institute of Religion, Cincinnati, for a similarly keen and insightful treatment of Jewish legal (halakhic) backgrounds to the play.

I am also deeply grateful to a number of people who have helped me, as is said in the old-new Hebrew idiom, "to bring the work into the light" of publication. Among these are: Rabbi David Stavsky of Congregation Beth Jacob of Columbus, Ohio, for his wise counsel on doctrinal matters pertaining to Leone's work; Rabbi Steve Abrams, Chaplain of the O.S.U. Bnai Brith Hillel Foundation, who offered his comment on the original translation and support for my endeavor; and Professor Christian Zacher, Director of the Center for Medieval and Renaissance Studies at Ohio State, who placed his own good offices and the resources of the Center at my disposal in the preparation of the manuscript. In both the play text and the Introduction, any errors, whether of omission or commission, found there certainly can not be attributed to them, but to me as translator and author.

To my dear wife Evelyn and dear sons Jeremy and Michael, I cannot convey in words my heartfelt thanks for being my "prop and stay" during the completion of this labor. Their presence and good wishes provided that warm and genial atmosphere needed for me to bring *A Comedy of Betrothal* to a fruitful conclusion.

The reader may be interested to know that an outgrowth of this "literary" translation has been an adaptation of the text of the play for modern audiences. The stage version of the play was presented in English for the first time at Temple Israel, Columbus Ohio, on February 27, 28 and March 1, 1988. The presentation of Leone's play as a *Purimspiel* in its original multi-media format was accomplished through the generosity of the Ohio State University, the Ohio Arts

Council/Ohio Humanities Council Joint Program, the Columbus Jewish Foundation, the Wexner Foundation and the Melton Center for Jewish Studies. Assisting me as director were my colleagues at O.S.U.'s College of the Arts: Professor Martha Maas, with her Collegium Musicum, who supplied authentic sixteenth century musical *intermezzi*; Professor Angelika Gerbes and her Historic Dance Ensemble, who provided Renaissance dance and choreography; and Professor Thomas Heck, who coached the singing and guitar accompaniment of Renaissance love lyrics. In this regard I am also most grateful to the artistry of Professor Russel Hastings of the Theatre Department for his scene sketches, Ms. Lisa Molyneux, a graduate of the same Department for her costume drawings, and Professor Scott Corliss for the lighting that illuminated both investiture and performers. The illustrations reproduced within this volume derive from the designs for the set by Professor Hastings and for the costumes by Ms. Molyneux.

Alfred S. Golding

INTRODUCTION

The Author, the Play and Its Staging

About the middle of the sixteenth century, a young Italian-Jewish playwright finished an unusual dramatic work. If its plot was reminiscent of Plautus and its characters of the commedia dell'arte, the language of its writing was Hebrew and its content Judaic. In his own way the author of *A Comedy of Betrothal* was as unique as his play. He had been reared in the Jewish community of Mantua in the orthodox tradition and made his living as a calligrapher of religious scrolls and documents. But from his teachers he had also received training in the humanism that pervaded all segments of Italian society—including those of the Hebrew faith. Within a few years Yehudah Sommo (as he was know to his co-religionists) or Leone de' Sommi, Hebreo (in his Gentile appellation) would be recognized as a gifted poet in the Hebrew language and a talented director of the levy of Jewish performers who regularly entertained the Gonzaga at their court.[1]

It is not accidental that the nurture of his talent occurred within the precincts of Mantua,[2] for that "joyous city" (*Qiryah'Alizah*, as it was termed in Hebrew) and its environs had become a vital center for the arts of Lombardy and northern Italy. Vasari spoke of Mantua as a "new Rome," and to it came for extended visits such luminaries as the Flemish painter Peter Paul Rubens and the composer Claudio Monteverdi. Driven to make the city a place of creativity and learning, Don Cesare Gonzaga in 1562 founded the Accademia dell'Invaghiti (in the fanciful language of the time the "Academy of the Lovesick"—for things artistic and intellectual). Two years later Pope Pius IV gave his blessing to the enterprise by agreeing to be its spiritual sponsor. Since membership in that august body automatically conferred knighthood upon its members, they were thereby allowed to wear the papal insignia incorporated into the Academy's coat-of-arms. Under the enlightened rule of Dukes Guglielmo (1550–1587) and Vicenzo I (1587–1612), an illustrious company of composers, artists and scholars joined its ranks, as the Dukes in the same spirit encouraged all their subjects to work for the city's welfare.

In so benevolent an atmosphere the Jews of Mantua flourished alongside their Gentile neighbors, although their circumstances were not free of anti-Semitic attack. In contrast most of Italian Jewry suffered severely at times under the repression imposed by the papacy during the crisis of the Counter-Reformation. But at Mantua the Jewish community was not seriously threatened for the most part, and so was able to absorb the yeasty ferment of the Renaissance without sacrificing their own sacred traditions. Rabbi David Provenzal, for example, was so inspired by the new learning that he proposed that a Jewish university be established in which his co-religionists could study the secular wisdom, which was offered at the nearby Universities of Pisa and Bologna, while absorbing higher Jewish learning—the study of the Torah, the Talmud and Responsa. Abraham Portaleone (of the same family as Leone de' Sommi) was a pioneer archaeologist in reconstructing the architecture of Solomon's Temple and its service, who also wrote extensively on the theory of rhetoric. His colleague, Judah Muscato, was a poet and orator who thrilled Mantuan audiences with the eloquence of his Italian declamation. So highly did the Gonzaga value the mental acuity and verbal gift of the mathematician and engineer Abraham Colorni, that they dispatched him on a delicate mission to Prague on their behalf. Salomone di Rossi, who composed liturgical music for the synagogue, was so admired by his Gentile neighbors that he was asked to contribute music to the public celebrations of city and court.[3] Nevertheless, with all the recognition accorded its men of talent, Mantuan Jewry was reminded of its inferior status by being required to wear in public the yellow patch upon their clothing that marked them as "faithless" Jews to observing Christians.

The irony of this social situation is distinctly seen in the way in which the community undertook to provide entertainment for the court theatricals. The history of Jews as entertainers dates back at least to the late Middle Ages, a time when Jews literally had to play the fool in the pre-Lenten carnival celebrations. As secular entertainment began to replace performances on religious themes, Jews of talent offered their services as actors, musicians and dancers for state and civic functions. At Mantua, Jews had been active as performers since the beginning of the sixteenth century. An official document of 1520 notes that Duke Ercole Gonzaga had invited two Jewish players, Solomon and Jacob, from Ferrara to perform before him. By 1525 the court archives reveal that Jews were regularly appearing upon the court stage, and in 1563 a troupe comprised mainly of Jews presented Ariosto's *Suppositi* ("the Supposes") at court in honor of the visit of Archdukes Rudoloph and Ernst of Austria. The Gonzaga apparently so appreciated the quality of Jewish performance that they mandated that the community supply the bulk of the actors and underwrite a great part of the large costs of production. Usually this levy was filled by volunteers, but occasionally community members had to be drafted. The Jewish quarter also, on occasion, would furnish the play, the music and the dance for the intermediary actions interspersing the acts, as well as the direction for these production elements, and, in addition, the scenic investiture, the lighting and the costume. Seemingly their efforts were highly appreciated, for the court decreed that the Jewish players did not have to perform on the Jewish Sabbath or holy days, an activity that would be in conflict with the tenets of their faith.[4] It may be presumed that this admiration was predicated on 1) the skill of the performers in rendering the complex roles of the *commedia erudita*, and 2) the fact that the members of the Jewish troupe were still amateurs (in the original sense of the word) who regularly worked at other pursuits, for Renaissance society accorded the dilettante player considerable respect.

For the most part Mantuan Jewry welcomed the chance to join with other townsmen in the pursuit of theatrical activity. The theatre, however, occupied a peculiar place in the Jewish historic memory. Almost two millennia earlier, following the absorption of the lands of the Near East into the Hellenistic Greek and the Roman Empires, the theatre edifice assumed a special significance in Levantine civic architecture. The stadium, hippodrome and circus represented the new dominant cosmopolitan civilization that ranged across the Mediterranean littoral, eradicating cultural differences by allowing all inhabitants to share in a common polity. Attendance at the entertainments that occurred within these structures was evidence that the populace had accepted not simply the regime's political authority, but its cultural and religious values as well. But to believing Jews of this world (and to their Christian contemporaries), often what passed for diversions within these structures was an affront to their most fundamental moral sensibility. To the Jewish soul, as was recorded in the Talmud then in the process of compilation, the bloody arena games were sacrilege. But the actions of the comedies—with light-minded men and women of easy virtue, and phallophoric slaves tickling an audience's erotic fancy, and the even more titillating scenes of mime and pantomime that featured explicit sexual congress—were considered no less abominable desecrations of the human spirit. Subsequent generations studying the Talmud from earliest childhood absorbed this same animadversion to anything theatrical, a sentiment still shared, as we have seen, by some in the Italian-Jewish community during the time of Leone.

I

The way out of this seeming impasse—between a tradition that sanctioned dramatic activity for Jewish holiday merrymaking, and another that condemned the drama as immoral—was to create a theatre that, while it entertained, would also convey authentic Jewish ethical values. The application of this ethical function to dramatic performance, however, was hampered for lack of a historic connection between theatre artistry and the Jewish heritage, as this was manifested in the Hebrew Bible, the Talmud and post-Talmudic literature. The need to affirm this liaison is readily evident in de' Sommi's writings on playmaking and in the plays themselves. It was a task that was both delicate and perilous, for well past his lifespan many notable leaders of Italian Jewry, like Rabbi Samuel Abuhav of Venice, continued to condemn even play performances that evinced Jewish themes.[5]

By background, training and temperament Leone de' Sommi was well fitted to the task. He was born about 1527[6] to Isaac de' Sommi of the distinguished Portaleone family that had long lived in Italy and produced generations of men active in public life, science and, particularly, medicine. (Several of his forebears were well-known physicians to the nobility of Naples, Urbino, Venice and Mantua.) His earlier religious and secular education was under the aforementioned Rabbi David Provenzal, who in his early years must have screened him from all contact with things theatrical. The boy Leone instead concentrated his energies upon the craft of writing, precociously translating at the age of eleven for his teacher the work of Ibn Ezra on rhetoric, *Sefer HaTsahut* ("The Book of Eloquence") into Italian. As a young man he first earned a modest living as a scrivener of religious texts, while writing poetry in Hebrew and in Italian in his spare time. One example of his poetic gift is his *Magen Nashim* ("A Defense of Women") in which Hebrew and Italian verses alternate in perfect rhythm and rhyme. The work was dedicated in typical romantic Renaissance fashion, to the wife of a good friend, the publisher Reuben Sullam. Public recognition of his felicitous Italian verse gave him access to the larger world beyond the Jewish quarter and ultimately brought him to the attention of the Mantuan court. Not yet forty, he received an invitation to join the Academy of the Lovesick that had been founded some four years earlier. But because it was deemed inappropriate for a Jew to be a knight who could bear the papal insignia upon his coat-of-arms, he received instead the inferior title of *scrittore* or scribe that was especially devised for him.

It was for the Academy that Leone did much of his fruitful work as poet, playwright and stage director. His pastorals, comedies and *intermezzi* were much desired for presentation at the court and civic festivals of his native city. Apparently he took charge of a number of these productions, for a letter from the poet Mutio Manfredi asks that Leone be the director of his work when it was to be presented before the Duke. The esteem of his Gentile contemporaries also finds reflection in the respect paid Veridico the theatre director by several noble gentlemen in Leone's insightful work on theatre staging, *Quattro dialoghi in materia di rappresentazione sceniche* ("Four Dialogues on the Art of Staging Plays"), written about 1565. The costumer Veridico is, of course, in Italian "the speaker of truth," the author's spokesman, and, implicitly, the "artisan" Leone himself. Yet it must be noted that while the artist was admired, there was prejudice against the Jew. In 1567, a year after his acceptance into the Mantuan Academy, Leone asked permission for himself to build and operate a public theatre in the city and so to employ his colleagues with whom he had worked in the earlier productions that had made his reputation. This permission the authorities denied, perhaps as well because the idea of a public theatre itself was too innovative and threatening to the court's prerogative. By 1580, however, his prestige and fortune had both increased to the extent that he was allowed to appear in public without the yellow patch that set him apart from non-Jews.[7]

Despite the eminence and the prosperity that he obtained from his theatrical employment, Leone remained a devoted member of the Jewish community. On a plot of land in Mantua that he acquired in 1585 he built a synagogue with the special permission of the Duke. His interest in the well-being of his co-religionists in Mantua and elsewhere remained firm, as numerous charitable documents attest. He died about 1592, in all likelihood in the city to which he had given so much of his talent.[8] His tombstone notes that such a one as Leone needs no mourning, for all his life he sought the welfare of his people and in his old age raised a synagogue; and these have become his memorial.

Leone left an extensive legacy of writings in Italian, most of which were eventually acquired by the Library of Turin. According to its catalogue, these consisted of four volumes of poems of different kinds, including a translation of the Psalms. Noteworthy also is the fact that the collection included some thirteen plays in poetry and in prose. These volumes, however, did not include the many shorter sketches and dialogues that he prepared for the carnival festivities of the court and the city of Mantua, which were to be found, as well, in the Turin collection. Unfortunately, in 1904 a great fire devastated the Turin Library and destroyed the de' Sommi holdings. Today there survives, of his Italian plays, only the *Hirifile* and the comedy *Le Tres Sorelle* ("The Three Sisters"), as well as fragments of other dramatic pieces. Happily, several of his poems and variant copies of his Hebrew play, *Tsahoth B'dihutha D'Kiddushin* ("A Comedy of Betrothal") were present in other libraries, as well as the *Quattro dialoghi in materia di rappresentazione sceniche*, and these also have come down to us.

II

It is certain that Leone's interest in dramatic performance was fostered by the theatricals staged to celebrate the Purim holiday and other notable occasions within the Jewish community, and there is good reason to believe that *A Comedy of Betrothal* was written as a *Purim-spiel*, the German-Jewish term for the Purim play. The late Professor J. Hayyim Schirmann, who was chiefly instrumental in discovering the play and attributing its authorship, believed that it was a youthful product of Leone's hand, written about 1550, or when the author was in his early twenties. By Jewish custom, Purim merry-making—like the Christian celebration of the pre-Lenten carnival—was improvised and the Italian-Jewish performers who enacted the traditional farce concerning the beautiful Queen Esther, her uncle the righteous Mordecai, and the villainous Haman at the court of the omnipotent but silly King Ahasuerus of Persia, did so in the free-wheeling *ad libitum* fashion of the popular commedia dell'arte. In such a performance, songs, dances and entertaining monologues were intermixed with the dialogue, together with jests made on subjects and personalities dear to the local community. The language of the performers was the Italian spoken by the local Jewish community, probably liberally salted with well-known Hebrew words and phrases. It is a reasonable conjecture that the revival of the ancient Latin plays by the Gentile academies, partly to glorify their own Roman ancestry, provided an example that the humanists in the Jewish quarter began to follow. Certainly during the course of the sixteenth century Jews began to compose plays in Hebrew for private reading and perhaps for public presentation before the more erudite. Although not used as a daily language by Italian Jewry, Hebrew functioned, much like the Neo-Latin of the period, as a language of scholarship and of oral communication with others from other parts of Europe who ordinarily spoke in a different vernacular tongue. So educated Jewish travellers, like their Christian counterparts in the language of Vergil and Cicero, could converse with their co-religionists using the word forms of the Bible and particularly the Talmud (which was particularly rich in the practical vocabulary of daily life). Because Jewish culture put a high price on literacy, the number of Italian Jews of the time who were Hebrew speakers was not inconsiderable. It is thus not surprising to find Joseph Sarfati of Rome, in the Renaissance spirit of the early sixteenth century, translating the *Celestina* from the Spanish of Fernando de Rojas (himself a Jewish convert to Catholicism). By the end of the same century in Mantua alone, the record reveals that a *Eunuchus in the Holy Language* (that is, the Terence play in Hebrew) had been printed, as well as *The Story of Joseph* (apparently a dramatization of the biblical narrative). It is notable that these plays were published in Mantua by Isaac Sullam, who also had printed one of the versions of *A Comedy of Betrothal* that Professor Schirmann had consulted in his reconstruction of the play.[9]

III

It is Schirmann's contention that *A Comedy of Betrothal* is by Leone de' Sommi and that it is the first Hebrew play that has come down to us in its more or less complete and original form. He thus claims Leone to be the founder of a subsequently developing Hebrew drama in Italy and elsewhere in Europe. However, as part of his argument, Schirmann has directed attention to the problems connected with the attribution of authorship, the originality of the play title and the variant nature of the texts that he employed in the reconstruction of the work. Four manuscripts of the play are extant, all dating from the early seventeenth century and in different hands. None clearly identifies the playwright, and it is problematic whether the lengthy Hebrew title itself (literally translated, "An Eloquent—or Stylish—Marriage Farce") attached to at least one manuscript version is the one bestowed by the original author. Schirmann argues as follows:[10]

1) He cites a manuscript dating from 1618 that contains, in its introduction, the words, "This is Yehudah's and this is what he said."

Within the intimacy of the Jewish quarter Leone was known by his
Hebrew name, Yehudah (Judah Sommo ben-Yitshaq (son of Isaac).
Among the Jews of Italy Yehudah was often rendered into a common vernacular Italian equivalent—Leone or lion, after the symbol
of the tribe of Judah ("Judah is a lion's whelp"—Exod. 49:9) Significantly, the same prefatory notice indicates that the play was
composed in the author's youth, which was many years before
the date of the handwritten copy. A second manuscript from the
early seventeenth century mentions that the play's author had died
a number of years before the copy was transcribed, and that he
had the secular name of "lion," that is, Leone in Italian.

2) Another primary text of the play contains a summary statement
drafted by the printer, Master Meshullam Sullam of Mantua. Schirmann feels that the location as well as the identity of the publisher
help in the identification of de' Sommi as the author. This published text is one of two that are of Mantuan provenance, and it
is Professor Schirmann's contention that a close connection existed between the publishing house owned by the Sullam family
and Leone. Schirmann cites, in this regard, the fact that in his
youth Leone had dedicated his bilingual poem, "A Defense of
Women," to Anna, the wife of Reuben Sullam, his friend, as we
have mentioned earlier.

3) Schirmann also adduces stylistic evidence—namely, that a number
of expressions found in the Hebrew play are strikingly like those
found in his known Italian works, poetic, dramatic and critical.
There seems as well to be a similarity in structure and content of
the Hebrew comedy with the desiderata for play form and substance found in Leone's *Dialogues*. Schirmann ascribes any minor
differences to the fact that the latter was written in the playwright's
maturity, while *A Comedy of Betrothal* was a youthful effort.

For these reasons Schirmann is convinced that *A Comedy of Betrothal* is an early dramatic work by Leone written when he was in
his mid-twenties—that is about 1550. That Leone actually gave his
play that title, he is less sure. The printer Isaac Sullam had made
copies of a play whose Hebrew title was *B'dihuta D'Kiddushin, heno
Komedya Ivri* ("A Marriage Farce, Which is A Comedy in Hebrew")
as a Mantuan registry of Jewish publications of 1595 indicates. Because of the near similarity of the title to later manuscripts in which
the play is called *Tsahut B'dihuta D'Kiddushin*, Schirmann feels that
this is unquestionably the same play. Because the registry seems to be

the earliest documented reference to the play, he argues by reason of recency, that Leone so entitled his play. This is to say that Schirmann recognizes the strong possibility that the subject of betrothal or marriage (*kiddushin* in Hebrew may designate both terms) was certainly in the original title. *Komedya*, however, may not have been. It was a loan word that had come into the Hebrew in the Greco-Roman period and may have possessed something of a pejorative connotation by association with the licentious theatre of the time. Hence Leone may have utilized the circumlocution *Tsahut B'dhuta* ("An Eloquent— or Stylish—Farce) to avoid the connection of "comedy" with vicious entertainment. Such speculation, Schirmann admits, may at best offer a suggestion of what his original title may have been, but hardly more than that.

Schirmann makes another argument to support his claim that Leone was the author of *A Comedy of Betrothal*, namely that in both the Hebrew play and the Italian work on play production, a direct appeal is made to quintessential Jewish sources to sanction theatrical presentation. In the former it is to the *midrash* or parable that is analogous to comedy in providing amusing instruction that reference is made. In the latter it is to the Book of Job that the reader is directed by way of dramatic model. In each instance the rhetorical appeal is similar. In each, also, there exists a comparable fervor with respect to the use of religious material as support for theatrical performance. Both appeals bespeak the impassioned scholar steeped in Jewish traditional learning, as well as the ardent *uomo di teatro*, versed in its arcane secrets. Within the sixteenth century, Schirmann affirms, certainly only in one man, Leone de' Sommi, Hebreo can scholars identify such dedication—both to the Torah and to the art of the theatre.

IV

Was Leone's justification for dramatic artistry simply a rationale-excuse according to the Horatian formula adopted by Renaissance play-making theorists for condoning comedic pleasure because it corrected vice? Schirmann notes that while this may have been partly true, Leone also made use of a traditional Jewish means for approving what was new and not fully accepted. This was by ascribing its authorship to ancient authority or by interpreting it metaphorically so as to invest it with the spirit of the old and established. An obvious example of such a method was the attribution to King Solomon of the authorship of Ecclesiastes and the Song of Songs by the compilers of the biblical canon.

Another example of almost the same antiquity is the recognition of the synagogue prayer service as a replacement for the sacrificial offering at the Temple in Jerusalem. In this fashion, as we have already seen, Leone seized upon a theory propounded by the sages of the Talmud that Moses the Lawgiver was the author of the Book of Job. Since Leone saw a striking resemblance in its structure and substance to ancient Greek tragic drama, and since in his view the story of Job preceded Greek tragedy, he concluded that the origin of the theatre lay not in Greece but in Israel. Similarly he justified comedic performance as but an extension of the aggadic homilies and witty proverbs for ethical instruction that studded Holy Writ.[11]

In this regard Leone's pronouncement of the Jewish origin of the theatre needs to be seen in the context of the time—as a need to reconcile the modern theatre with traditional values and customs. In saying so, however, we must also recognize the strong moral element that is present in his Hebrew play.[12] If Leone did not provide clear solutions to the several problems of contemporary Italian Jewish life, he did give them fair definition. In fact, the theme of *A Comedy of Betrothal* resonates with the complex ethical and legal issues that were the traditional subject of Jewish scholarly debate. In this sense Leone extended the customary dialectical study of the Jewish Academy (*Yeshivah*) to the theatrical arena. Implicit in the play are such Talmudic imperatives as: contracts are not to be broken, young women are not to be manipulated for private gain or selfish ends. Moreover, as a Purim play there is also present an over-arching social theme: if there is to be redemption from Gentile oppression, the Jewish community must itself be free of domestic wrongdoing.

Although his substance was Jewish, Leone subscribed to a Roman comedic form, as did his Renaissance contemporaries. Emulating Plautus, he divided his work into five separate "parts," as he called his acts (*heleq* in the Hebrew singular), each of which he further divided into "colloquies" (*dibbur* is his Hebrew word for scene). The play's sequence of actions closely follows the formula for plotting that he set out in his *Dialogues*: an exposition of the situation and the impending conflict; further complication of the comedic circumstances; followed, in turn, by a relaxation of the tension of conflict; only to result in a climax, by way contrast; and, finally, an unexpected denouement.[13] Within this plot arrangement he holds to a unity of place and, with some latitude, of time: nearly all the action occurs in a piazza in Sidon before the houses of the three principal characters; similarly, one scene flows into another without interruption within an indefinite time interval that may be from twenty-four to thirty-six hours in duration. The characteristic shape of the plot is that of the *contamnatio*, of Greco-Roman provenance, in which separate story lines intertwine to create an increasingly complex skein of twists and turns of events. These plot strands Schirmann correctly identifies as four in number:

1) The love relationship of young Jedidiah and Beruriah. Because the young man's father has died suddenly while abroad and left his considerable fortune to his slave rather than to his son, the young girl's parents betroth her, although she is not aware of the fact, to another young man of solid substance and background. With his faithful serving man, Jedidiah secretly follows her to the country where she has been sent to escape his attentions. There he seduces her in order to compel her parents to acknowledge the betrothal according to the Jewish legal principle of "marriage by intercourse." Brought to trial on capital charges for seducing a virgin, Jedidiah defends himself by declaring that as Beruriah's legally espoused he was potentially her husband—hence there was no rape. Because the first betrothal contract was still binding, the second was invalid. The plot strand is based upon a similar action found in Ariosto's *Lena* (1525).

2) The Asael-Beruriah ploy. Asael, a son of Ephron, a neighbor, is interested in Shifrah, the sister of Jedidiah, who has been living with Beruriah in her parents' household, since Shifrah's father had gone abroad. This interest Beruriah's parents, Amon and Deborah, mistakenly believe is directed toward their daughter, and so after the news of Shifrah's and Jedidiah's father's death is received, they resolve to have her wed Asael and so to rid themselves of an apparently embarrassing commitment. Without consulting Beruriah, Amon arranges a betrothal ceremony to be held. Bewildered by the rush of events, Beruriah does not understand what is taking place and so does not object to the ceremony. Here the plot hinges on a piece of Jewish law that requires participants in a betrothal contract to enter of their own free will and to be cognizant of what they are doing—women as well as men.

   In contrast to the first, the second strand derives directly from the Jewish experience.

3) The action centering upon Master Greedy, a lawyer. Prior to the events of the play, Greedy had pocketed funds entrusted to him by Ephron's late brother for distribution to the poor of the community.

But as executor of the will of the decedent, Greedy declares to
Ephron that he will only do so providing Asael, Ephron's son, becomes Greedy's son-in-law. Ephron, in the course of the play, has
Asael pretend to betroth himself to one of Greedy's two daughters
but, slyly, without specifying which (a requirement of the Jewish
marriage code). So hasty is the lawyer to enter into a liaison with
one of Sidon's first families that he fails to notice this important
omitted detail. Only after he has returned the withheld money
does he realize that the betrothal contract is not legally binding
and that he has been duped. This plot also is rooted in Jewish life
where respect for principles of law was valued as the means of
preserving domestic concord and ensuring social justice.

4) The Shovel action. Linking this strand to the other plot lines is
the fact that Shovel, a former slave who has become heir to his
wealthy master's property, wishes to marry the younger daughter
of Master Greedy. Greedy, however, is unaware from Shovel's
present ostentatious dress and manner that he had formerly been a
slave—in fact to Jedidiah's deceased father. But, as the venerable
Rabbi Amitai points out, a proviso in the latter's will stipulates
that Jedidiah can pick one small piece of his father's estate as
his inheritance. The young man thereupon chooses Shovel, and
so receives his full inheritance according to the principle that the
master of a slave is also master of the slave's property. A similar
story is found in Midrash Tanhuma.

The marriage of Renaissance structure and Jewish content that
informed the plot of *A Comedy of Betrothal* may also be detected in
Leone's delineation of its characters. As did his Gentile contemporaries, Leone drew upon an already established typology of Roman
provenance that, nevertheless, was invested with Renaissance features.
Following the models provided by the erudite comedy and the commedia dell'arte, Leone gave his characters the features of everyday Italian
life—the patrician merchant-masters of the city-state, their families and
servants. But in his Hebrew comedy these become an individualized
portraiture of Jewish community life. Although removed in time to
antiquity and in space to Sidon, Phoenicia, the characters are recognizable as Jews of Leone's time, no less by their behavior than by their
dress and the architecture of their environment. It is from this background that the satire of the play emerges. Here are the bergamasks of
a Jewish carnival play who live just outside the bounds of Israel but
who are patently Mantuans. They are under the benevolent protection

of a Gentile Duke (Gonzaga), who allows the community control of its internal affairs and who assists his Jewish subjects in the administration of justice, although under Jewish law. In so optimal a climate they can only thrive and prosper—providing they can deal justly and mercifully with each other. For as is implicit in the play, albeit in a comedic way, it is possible for otherwise decent folk to act tyrannically when they do not follow time-honored Law. Thus it is not accidental that the well-meaning but weak Amon becomes Haman, and Master Greedy turns into vice personified, when according to the Prologue, they do not walk in the path of Wisdom. To make his moral statement, Leone has deliberately given his human figures something of a symbolic cast, while endowing his allegorical figure Wisdom with some human warmth. His characterization, therefore, does not lean heavily upon a humors psychology, although of all his characters, Leone has patterned Master Greedy, the most extreme deviant from the social norm, after the Galenic behavior theory.

An analysis of the individual characters confirms their hybrid makeup. Yet the severity of their eccentricities is tempered by their inherent, if momentarily dormant, ethicality. None is so evil that he cannot be reformed, or so foolish that he cannot be made wiser by proper teaching. That ethic is evident in the shaping of their *personæ* and their names.

Amon heads the list of dramatic figures. He is the traditional patrician and *paterfamilias* of Italian comedy, and something of a Pantalone as well. His name is carefully chosen for a major character in a *Purimspiel*: in its pronunciation it sounds much like Haman, particularly so in the pronunciation of the Italian Jew who tended to omit the initial aspirant ("H") in Hebrew as well as in Italian. But Amon also reminded the *literati* in the audience of the wicked king of scriptures, although the character Amon is not deliberately wicked, only easily led. "Amon," in one sense, can mean in Hebrew "gullible" or "capable of believing," and its root is related to the "amen" (in Hebrew, "so let it be believed") of Jewish and Christian prayer. Hence the character of Amon is that of one who accedes, perhaps too readily, to a person of stronger mind—in this case his wife Deborah. A man of substance, he, like Pantalone, is too given over to the treasuring of money, and this attitude figures in the near-disastrous consequences set in motion when he arbitrarily cancels Jedidiah and Beruriah's betrothal contract.

As a foil, Leone has introduced the person of Ephron, also a patrician and a family-father, but a man of balance and good judgement.

He swiftly rises (like the lark, which his name means in Hebrew) to challenge the knavery of Master Greedy. In his upright dealings with honorable men and his ability to use appropriate countermeasures against a devious opponent, he stands as a counterpart to the behavior of Amon, his neighbor.

Deborah is Amon's overbearing wife, who alternately employs a scolding tongue and honeyed words to get what she wishes from her husband. In Hebrew, Deborah means "bee," and like the insect Deborah can sting and "sweet-talk" those about her.

Jedidiah is another of the young, handsome and somewhat unworldly lovers who populate Renaissance Italian comedy. As his Hebrew name implies he is divinely favored, having been born into a wealthy family and having received a proper Jewish education. Thus, he should be ready to manage his own affairs. But his passionate desire for Beruriah and the shock of his father's sudden death and being left penniless—deprive him of the ability to think sensibly. In this regard he is the typical *inamorato* of the *Rinascimento*, "sighing like furnace with a woeful ballad made to his mistress' eyebrow." But he is also recognizable as a Torah scholar—indeed an advanced student of the venerable Rabbi Amitai. This combination of Gentile and Jewish qualities was not at all the incongruity to a Mantuan Jewish audience that it may seem to us today, for as we have hitherto observed, to some extent it was possible for Italian Jews to live in a Gentile as well as Jewish world during the sixteenth century.

The character of Beruriah, the daughter of Amon and Deborah, has the same curious dualism as does Jedidiah. Like her *inamorata* counterparts of the *commedia*, she is madly in love with her suitor, but unlike most of them, she is modest and chaste. Wan and sick with grief at being parted from her lover, she is a victim both to the unscrupulousness of her parents and the rashness of her beloved. Her Hebrew name bespeaks her character: "G-d's purity."

Asael is, in effect, the second *inamorato* of the play, in love with Shifrah, sister to Jedidiah, although he never appears on the stage. In his calm and straightforward demeanor, he is in sharp contrast to his fellow-student and friend, the emotional and romantic Jedidiah. Asael is a dutiful son to Ephron and follows his father's wishes even at the risk of imperiling his own suit for Shifrah's hand. His name in Hebrew means "G-d has wrought," and is emblematic of Asael's balanced, practical nature.

Pash-hur is Jedidiah's faithful servant, an energetic man of apparent approaching middle age who would prefer a quiet life to one of adventure. He is in some ways the traditional Pedrolino—a pivotal figure who must provide the practical advice for his unworldly young master and be a friend-in-need in his adversity. Yet in the *commedia* tradition, he is also a bit of a rogue and *bon-vivant* as well as being whey-faced and ordinarily cowardly. But so devoted is he that he dares to be brave in his master's cause. His name in Hebrew exemplifies his essential trait, "foolish," or in another sense, "pale of face."

His female counterpart is Jekarah, the maidservant in Amon's household who is devoted to Beruriah. She is a variation of an altogether familiar comedic type who is, like the nurse in *Romeo and Juliet*, at once dedicated to the welfare of her mistress, at times self-centered, slippery and coarse and at times intimate and tender. Unlike the usual *commedia* plot convention in which the love affair of master and mistress finds a rude parallel in that of man- and maidservant, here Leone has her rebuff Pash-hur's advances. She, perhaps even more than Pash-hur, has a humanity that gives the servant role an unusual dignity. Her name, again in a literal and ironic sense, can mean "Deary" or "Precious" to an audience knowledgeable of Hebrew.

Shovel is the former companion of Pash-hur, a servant who has risen in life by inheriting his master's wealth. He now flaunts his new riches but cannot disguise the oaf underneath the finery. He is swollen with the pride of possession, but is ignorant of how to use it wisely. His name conveys this idea, again in metaphoric terms in Hebrew: "a rich robe," or more precisely," the train of a noble's garment."

Master Greedy is the conventional pseudo-learned doctor-of-laws of the Italian popular comedy transmuted into the law practitioner of the Jewish quarter. He hails not from the distinguished University of Bologna, a center since medieval times for legal study, but from the Galilee, a region noted for Talmudic scholarship in Jewish law in the Greco-Roman period. As the prime villain of the piece who nevertheless is a source of merriment, Master Greedy is perhaps the most fascinating of Leone's characters. His legal knowledge is not thorough or profound, but he is proficient in many small details of practice. He also has a quick mind which he employs to his own rather than his client's complete advantage. His vitality, coupled with a disarming private candor when explaining his own motives in asides to the audience, provokes laughter that is not entirely unsympathetic. Manifestly he is a charming shyster whose services, Leone stresses, are in constant demand by the public. But he is not simply a harmless

aberrant from the social norm; as Leone has drawn him, he can be a
potential threat to the welfare of the community. Indeed, given the
cleverness that he displays earlier in pulling off shady legal dealings,
his final comeuppance through his failure to detect the stratagems of
Ephron and Rabbi Amitai seems somewhat contrived. As in Molière's
Tartuffe, are we to understand that an arbitrary ending has been planned
as a warning to the audience not to dismiss too lightly the danger posed
by such a man? Significant also in this regard is that, of all the *dramatis
personae*, Greedy most clearly resembles those cast from the mold of
an increasingly popular humors psychology. For this reason—and so
that modern readers may become aware of what was patent to Leone's
audience—I have provided the English equivalent of the character's
name in Hebrew, that of "Hamdan"—"Greedy." The root of the word,
Leone's audience recognized, was the same as that found in the second
word of the Tenth Decalogue, *Lo Tahmod!*, usually translated as "Thou
Shalt Not Covet!" In this respect, too, it is well to note that while
all the characters have authentic Biblical or Talmudic names (chosen,
of course, for their symbolic meaning), "Hamdan" is an out-and-out
attribute, conceived in much the same way and for the same purpose
that Ben Jonson did Volpone or Mosca.

A uniquely Jewish creation is the character of the Venerable Rabbi
Amitai. He is all the things that Master Greedy is not: a genuinely
erudite scholar—one vastly learned in the intricacies of the Torah, a
saintly man yet knowledgeable of the ways of the world and the human
heart. He is the spirit of wisdom of the piece and, in a sense, its *deus
ex machina*, for in the finale it is the revelation of his original plan that
ties up the separate strands and ends the action. His name in Hebrew
can mean "Truth-bringer."

The young lads Jair and Joktan as characters provide occasional
comic relief, but are not indispensable to the plot. They are apprentices
in the household of Master Greedy and take full advantage of his being
too busy to fulfill his contractual obligation to their parents to give them
basic instruction in the law. Instead, they are left largely to their own
devices and pass the time in gaming and gluttony. Their names may
loosely be translated as "Bright-eyes" and "Tiny."

Obed, whose name in Hebrew means servant or slave, is of that
lowest social position. This is particularly humiliating when he must
serve his former companion, Shovel. Obed's is thus a somewhat tragi-
comic role, for he has more common sense than his new master, which
nevertheless he cannot disguise and so provokes Shovel by talking to

him as if he were Obed's equal. Though a small role, the character has
a subtlety that springs from the tension existing between a freed slave
and another who is treated in a servile manner so that the freedman
can display his fancied superiority.

Although the symbolism inherent in the names of Obed and the
other figures of the drama provide clues to their natures, it is in their
actions that their characters are fully revealed. In so stating, however,
we should also recognize that physical activity is at a minimum in the
comedy. Only two scenes feature what may be termed in today's stage
parlance, "business" for visual theatrical effect. Thus in Act I, Scene
4, Pash-hur makes ribald advances upon Jekarah who just as deftly
defends her honor; and in Act IV, Scene 1 Pash-hur loses his temper
and proceeds in a ludicrous fashion to knock about Shovel and Obed,
who are too clumsy and cowardly to protect themselves. Interestingly,
both scenes exhibit the characteristics which made the Italian popular
comedy famous: sketchy, even fragmented dialogue that was contrived
to set off the equally farcical *lazzi* or stage business.

Still, particularly in the Pash-hur-Jekarah love-duel, what verbal
repartée there is, is quite witty and resembles in its conceits, many
another such scene framed by other dramatists of the time.

With the exception, therefore, of these two scenes, Leone has
emphasized the dialogue at the expense of physical action. By doing
so he reveals his willingness, insofar as is possible, to conform to the
academic rules for playmaking: a compression of the incidents of the
play to fit within the dimensions of a single time and place; and the
fusing of the four plot strands into a single cable of action insofar as
they reflect a common theme—the impropriety of making wealth the
major criterion in matchmaking. In consequence, Leone does not show
to his audience earlier or concurrent events that occur elsewhere, but
must describe them in often elegant Hebrew prose. So in Act II, Scene
3 he has Ephron expose his previous inability to compel Greedy to
disburse the charity money, Jedidiah his tryst with Beruriah in Act IV,
Scene 5 and Asael in Act IV, Scene 1 the attack made upon his life
by his supposed friend Jedidiah—all scenes in themselves of highly
stageworthy activity.

What becomes clear is that through his verbal emphasis, Leone is
suggesting that the language that he employs has a character no less allusive than the metaphoric nature of his plotting and characterization.[14]
Moreover, from a dramatic vantage point the dialogue can be seen to
stem from the traits with which he has endowed his dramatic figures

and the conditions in which he has placed them. This mix charges the dialogue and propels it forward. The speeches by the characters, if not unusually idiosyncratic, are nonetheless determined by their psychological makeup, and by such factors as age, sex and social position— significant distinctions during the Renaissance. Servants did not talk like their masters, nor children like adults, nor, indeed, women like men in the formulas of Renaissance rhetoric. Within these categories, Leone assigns a certain degree of distinctiveness to his figures that is evident in their speeches. By conforming to the classic dictum of limiting the number of personages that may appear on the stage at any one time, Leone forces into prominence these differences in language. The result is that the invariably conflicting views of the characters are enhanced and form a dialectic of often highly dramatic effect. Even the retrospective soliloquies demonstrate a similar, interesting debate as the characters inwardly struggle to decide which of several courses of action they should take.

The dramatic effectiveness of the dialogue is also evident in a style which is neither so spare and laconic as to be dull, or so ornately figured as to be obscure or hard to follow. When he uses allusion to ornament his dialogue, he uses Hebrew metaphor that would be well-known to a Bible-reading audience. His sentence organization is seldom involved; even where there are structural inversions, these are relatively free of syntactical complications or tangential *obiter dicta*. It is a rhetoric of public address that is manifest in his prose, a manner designed for oral delivery and aural comprehension.

Perhaps because he was a scholar of the written word, Schirmann seems not to have had an ear for the quality of spoken dialogue, for he does not discuss this feature of Leone's Hebrew in any great detail. Yet to the student of rhetoric or acting there is discernible in the original language of the play a natural cadence that is found in good theatre speech, but not necessarily in work meant to be read silently. Conforming to the classic precepts for comedy, he wrote the play in prose—although he was perfectly capable of writing metric verse, as his other poetry demonstrates. The dictum which he followed was that comedy, being concerned with the life of burgherdom, should not take on the elevated, metrified tone of the speech of the nobility, who were the central actors in tragedy. The fact that the diction of the original Hebrew is styled for speaking becomes another argument to support Schirmann's claim that the play was performed.

If he does not adduce the evidence of a speaking style in this regard, Schirmann does refer to statements within the text and information generally known about Jewish community performance[15] to prove that the play was at least written to be performed—and probably was performed both during the author's lifetime and for some years afterward. The principal documentation that he offers to demonstrate that the play was not a closet drama derives from the Prologue. Here Wisdom proclaims that the play is to be "laughed at," and that it is to be directed to "friendly listeners"—that is to an audience (not readers!) disposed to be entertained at holiday time. Several references within the text itself point to the fact that it is a Purim play—that is, meant to be offered as part of that holiday's religiously required public rejoicing. From our knowledge of the sixteenth-century Italian-Jewish community and its playmaking proclivities, we know that such plays were most often written in Italian, but sometimes in Hebrew. From our information of Italian-Jewish dramatic writing of the seventeenth and eighteenth centuries, we know, as well, that Hebrew plays were regularly presented by that time both in Italy and in Germany. It is therefore likely, as Schirmann contends, that Leone's play was one of these early experiments. Schirmann presents a final confirming argument: that the second variant manuscript of the play, preserved from the seventeenth century, contains the statement that the play was performed "afresh" before an audience, hence lending credence to the idea that an earlier version was actually played in public.[16]

V

There are grounds, therefore, to believe that *A Comedy of Betrothal* was written to be enacted. If such is the case, then we may well ask, where and how was it staged? Though we lack direct confirmation of the time and place of the première, we may nevertheless make some attempt at a theoretical reconstruction based upon what we know about Renaissance staging practice, especially as many details of this information are supplied by Leone himself.[17] Important in our reconstruction is the weight that Leone placed upon symbolism and allegorical representation in crafting theatrical performance—an emphasis that pervades his treatise on play production and runs like a *leitmotif* through the text of his comedy.

We must pause briefly in our reconstruction of the circumstances of the staging at this point to enlarge upon the use of symbolism as a fundamental element in the nature of Renaissance theatre artistry, for only in the last decades have scholars given it close attention and

the phenomenon is still not clearly understood. Certainly it was not
adequately recognized by Schirmann in his pioneering labors to restore
the play text and to identify its author. Schirmann, if nothing else,
was a perceptive *Theaterwissenschaftler* of his time, imbued with the
spirit of philosophic naturalism that dominated theatre historiography
during the first decades of the twentieth century and gave rise to "sci-
entific" theatre research. For him, as for most of his contemporaries,
the allegorical personages, scenes, ballets and musical compositions
that studded the performance of an Italian Renaissance drama were
understandable as vestigial remnants of late medieval theatre practice.
Symbolic materials, whether located within a play text or between its
performed acts was, in this naturalistic view, at best tangential to the
play, at worst thematically and structurally unconnected, but introduced
to satisfy an Italian audience's love of display. Corroboration for such
a position, as Schirmann himself points out, was found in Leone's own
statement that *intermezzi* were needed to provide the jaded spectator
with a refreshing change of scene. Considered from the naturalistic
point of vantage, symbolic action upon the stage was an intrusion into
the logical plotting, motivated characterization and illusionistic scenery
that were the hallmarks of Renaissance dramatic expression, the further
development of which led to the naturalistic playwriting of the early
twentieth century.

Today, however, we are beginning to recognize that Renaissance
theatricality transcended the representation of off-stage reality. Instead
it sought to convey a sense of the order underlying natural phenomena
by presenting in the guise of lifelike illusion a web of congruent figures
of speech, action and stage decoration, in much the same way as did
an iconological emblem. Through their analogical congruence these
symbolic elements resonated with a common but hidden theme, which
when amplified by juxtaposition within the framework of performance,
became apparent to the audience. The threading of metaphoric embroidery upon a dramaturgic fabric that was both highly realistic and
yet heavily figured with allegory, gave significance to the poetic and
allusive in the playmaking design.[18] This same literal-figurative tendency is evident in the recommendations of Veridico, the embroiderer
and fabricator, as to the way in which scenery and costume are to be
designed and the actor is to perform to reveal an otherwise concealed
truth (*verum*). Such verisimilitude is to be represented by action that on
one level follows the linear "cause-and-effect" logic that gives the appearance of daily life, and on another level that relates the performance

elements to each other by virtue of the fact that they are analogically similar.

Veridico-Leone's views on play production as a poetic construct were directed to a court theatre, manifestly a locale far different in its grand scale, sumptuous furnishing and elaborate machinery from the modest arena where Mantuan Jewry put on its holiday plays. We may justly surmise that no great hall resembling that of the ducal palace was located within the Jewish quarter, and it is hardly conceivable that any similar space outside the area would be let to the community, considering the repressive measures taken against it by a hostile Catholic church. In confirmation of this idea, we may note that even after Leone had gained wealth and reputation, the Mantuan authorities ë denied his petition to build a public theatre (that is, a hall properly designed and equipped for staging theatrical performances), and to operate it within the Jewish quarter.[19] Under such constraints, it is probable that *A Comedy of Betrothal* was first presented in some large room regularly given over to Jewish merrymaking. While Italian Jewry may have imitated their Gentile neighbors in celebrating some of their holidays out of doors, Purim was not likely to be one of them. Since it occurs on the 14th day of the Hebrew month of Adar, an early spring month falling in February and March, the weather of Cis-Alpine Italy is still too cool and rainy for extended outdoor celebration, and likely to damage delicate scenery and costuming.

We are probably on safer ground in projecting the première as occurring within a large indoor enclosure. Since the leaders of the Mantuan Jewish community, with their Gentile neighbors, prided themselves on their learning in classical subjects, we may presume that the structure of the stage and its appurtenances was in the latest fashion, as well as the configuration of seating for the audience. We know that under the influence of the Roman Academy and its successors, fashionable audiences sat at some modest distance, at least, from the playing area, and it is likely that this means for gaining aesthetic distance was followed here as well. Two possibilities exist for this seating configuration. The first is the amphitheatre-shape made famous in 1545 by Serlio in his *Architecture*, that reproduced the general practice employed in northern Italy. Such a disposition may not have been practical within the hall used by the Jewish community, for it demanded a tall ceiling to accommodate the height of the amphitheatre and the angle wings upon the stage. It is more probable that the spectators sat upon benches placed upon the floor, and perhaps as well, in loggia-boxes that were raised above the heads of the other spectators and ran about the rear and sides of the room. Apart from being a contemporary Italian seating practice, the disposition also corresponded to the seating that was customary in the synagogue, where men sat on ground level and women in a separate raised balcony at the rear and sometimes along the sides of the chamber. We may surmise that, to provide better visibility for the spectators seated on the ground level, the stage was raised several feet off the floor.

While Leone in the person of Veridico clearly opts for a Serlian perspective stage in his *Dialogues* as the background for the performance of tragedies, comedies and pastorals, it is conjectural whether this mode of scenography would have been used in the staging of *A Comedy of Betrothal*. Certainly it was one of three possible configurations that were in use about the middle of the sixteenth century, the others being either an unbroken or a broken line of booth-arcades representing a row of houses. The Serlian perspective was formed of angle wings to represent the various houses radiating up the stage to where a backdrop painted in perspective continued the street illusion. The booth-arcade, fitted with doorways for each of the houses of the main characters of the play, stood just upstage of the acting area. Behind this scene row was placed a painted backcloth of a town, or curtains masking the rear and side walls of the stage area.

Of these scenic alternatives, the Serlian illusion stage was the most modern. It was also, without doubt, the most expensive to build, and for this reason alone, singularly unpolitic for the Mantuan Jewish community to mount upon the stage. For, as Leone himself notes in his Fourth Dialogue, to expend money lavishly was a sign of princely magnanimity, and it would not have been prudent for the Jewish community, still near the bottom of the social scale despite the tolerance of the Gonzaga, to compete in the theatrical arena with its "betters." Hence we may suspect that the more circumspect row of booths was utilized. These were far more simple to build and were far less costly. Also the community was comfortable with them for they had been in use upon the stages of the academic theatres for more than half a century, and had been seen in the street pageantry of the Gentiles for an even longer period of time.

From the evidence within the text of Leon's play, strictly speaking only one house had to appear on stage—that of Amon's; however, the principle of the unity of place demanded that a locale be presented that could accommodate all the action involving the major characters.

To enhance the probability of this occurring, two other houses had to be shown—Ephron's home and that of Master Greedy, the foci, as it were, of the four major plots. Were the Serlian perspective used, conventional stage protocol (itself derived from classical and medieval usage),[20] dictated that the house of Amon, the most important of the three, be situated in the more significant position at downstage right. The weaker (and more sinister, literally and figuratively) would be given to the domicile of Master Greedy at downstage left. Ephron's home would then be represented by the second painted angle wing protruding from stage right immediately upstage of Amon's. Were, however, the booth-row used instead as the stage setting, the same protocol would place Amon's house at center stage (the most prominent position), Ephron's house on its right (the next position of importance), and Greedy's house on its left (of the three places the least important). To a Renaissance artist the latter arrangement would be perhaps more satisfying aesthetically than the former, since it would provide a direct correspondence between the significance of the proprietors of these households and the relative "valence" (aesthetic weight) conventionally assigned to the several stage areas. If the booth-houses were distinctly separated from each other, this effect would become pronounced.

In such a case, Amon's house at center stage could be built as a threefold scenic unit, a familiar early sixteenth-century scenic form. The threefold would comprise a large flat-frame with two smaller pieces hinged one on each side to angle upstage and so suggest the front facade and side walls of a building. Ephron's and Greedy's houses would also be formed of a large flat frame facing the audience, but each with a side piece joined to their on-stage sides and angled upstage to give depth to the building illusion. If these three scenic units were to be backed by a cloth drop painted in perspective, the illusion of a Renaissance town could be enhanced by reason of the angled walls and spaces between them that suggest streets that are continued in the painting on the backdrop.[21] If the painted backcloth was not used, for reasons of prudence or economy (as has been earlier mentioned), a curtain or neutral hanging would have been employed to mask the rear wall of the stage from the audience's view.

In what architectural style were these buildings rendered and how were they decorated to suggest an illusion of lifelikeness? Since the locale of the play is Sidon on the coast of Phoenicia, did the scenic artist attempt to duplicate the Levantine manner of architecture actually found in that geographic area?

Unquestionably we may assert that the scenic design for the première of *A Comedy of Betrothal* followed the classicistic tendency apparent in the paintings of Bramante and Peruzzi and summarized in the
scenography of Serlio. Such a style was not only modish, but, as we
have earlier suggested, the classicistic ideal had been embraced by the
leaders of Mantuan Jewry who saw in its humanism the ultimate possibility of living in concord with their Gentile neighbors, a condition
hinted at in the community's relatively good relations with the Gonzaga, a family strongly under the influence of the Renaissance spirit.
For this reason it is certain that the play's settings were not built in the
Turkish fashion that then dominated the Near East. It is quite possible, nevertheless, that touches of the Byzantine mode were present in
the architecture, for this style was part of the Veneto building design
that by the middle of the sixteenth century had crept westward from
Venice into Lombardy and Mantua. But, allowing for this Byzantine
flavor, we may suppose reasonably that the ideal underlying the scenic
decoration conformed to the same ideal of verisimilitude that lay at
the base of the play's dramaturgy—one that emphasized the symbolic
and the universal in preference to historical or geographical accuracy
in representation.

We may then state with some justification that the style of architecture used in the buildings that were represented on stage was some
simple adaptation of the Roman revival then popular in the structures
of the rich and powerful of the time. It was a style, moreover, which
admirably suited the message of the play, for Leone was revealing
in his comic vision not simply a world of timeless, universal beauty,
but one that contained imperfect human beings—in which Jewish patricians living in luxurious mansions in the latest fashion, blinded by
their wealth, did not see and take ethical courses of action.

The rational ethic of the humanistic vision produced a correspond-
ing logical geometry in the way architecture was designed and decorated, for to the Renaissance mind such formal arrangement signaled
an orderly world whose principles, like those of Euclid, were discov-
erable and usable for man's civil purposes. So Leone's setting would
have imitated the regular symmetry of contemporary Renaissance town
houses. To present the appearance of dressed stonework, cornices and
other ornamental forms, the flat-frames were painted in *trompe l'oeil*
fashion supplemented with the application of three dimensional mold-
ing in wood or plaster.

Renaissance costuming for the theatre subscribed to the same humanistic vision, and we may suppose that the dress worn by the actors in the première performance was selected according to the principles that emanated from that view. Leone no doubt intended that his characters represent not specific Mantuan Jews, but types that were general to the Jewish, and indeed the Gentile, population. It was for this reason that he removed the setting to a remote time and place. To make this statement plain, as did other costumers of his time, he made use of quotidian modes of dress that set apart master from serving man. This convention of daily life he made more pronounced to make stage costume more dramatically effective.[22] The manner of dress of Leone's characters, like the style of their houses, emulated the ways of the Gentile patricians, to whose social level the Mantuan Jewish merchants and bankers aspired.

We may reasonably conclude that Leone selected distinctive pieces of apparel of the time that could be used to clearly distinguish the men of wealth, a wife and daughter of one of them, the youths of rank and breeding, the canny lawyer and his apprentices, and the several sorts of servants. Today we may note that such distinctions in dress would be more difficult to make with the fading of class differences and the adoption of a more uniform apparel for rich and poor that can be almost indistinguishable except for those with an eye for fine material and tailoring. But the dress code of the sixteenth century tended to make outerwear homogeneous within social ranks so as to deliberately contrast one group with another and so make them readily identifiable. Because this was so common a phenomenon, it was apparently taken for granted. In consequence, in his Third Dialogue Leone did not need to refer to the readily evident protocols that made for class distinctions in dress, but only to show how to make such apparel more theatrical.

The costumes of *A Comedy of Betrothal*, then, were likely patterned on the fashionable dress of the mid-sixteenth-century Mantuan upper classes, and not that of Sidon of biblical antiquity, in order to dramatize the fact that the play is dealing with characters of the present day. In support of this contention we know that other playwrights in Italy and Europe during the sixteenth century observed that practice.[23]

But what are we to make of Leone's description that Beruriah's trousseau was to contain, among other articles, a "turban and sash"—typical Near Eastern garments? We may argue here that for want of Hebrew words to denote the specific articles of sixteenth-century dress, he made use of an older Biblical and Talmudic vocabulary to designate similarly appearing garments. Thus Beruriah could wear a headdress

and waistband of the sort worn by genteel young women as depicted
in contemporary painting—garments that could readily be described by
the terms "turban and sash" (in Hebrew, *mitsnefeth v'avnet*).[24]

We are safe in assuming that while Leone's *pronunciamentos* for
costuming (found in his Third Dialogue) held for court productions,
they were less likely to be mandated in a special Purim performance.
As with scenery, the community whose welfare depended in great part
upon the court's pleasure would not put itself at risk by surpassing the
costumes which it provided for the court in its own private theatricals.
Despite this caution we can believe that its Purim costuming was not
created shabbily or carelessly, but simply kept within the bounds of
prudence on one hand and connoisseurship on the other. *A Comedy
of Betrothal*, after all, was to reflect in a modest way, not rival in its
investiture, the presentations of the court theatre. It is in this spirit that
we must view the play's première.

It is with this same attitude also that we must regard the production's lighting. In common with other comedies of the period whose
dramaturgy derived from Renaissance academic interpretation of Aris-
totle, the play does not specifically identify the hours of the day: Leone
fitted his work into a timeless day during which the incidents could occur with some reasonable probability. Within this broad compass of
time, however, it would be quite possible to vary the levels of illumination required for sheer visibility to suggest the early light of morning,
a waning day and twilight, or even nighttime; or to change the inten-
sity and perhaps even color to accommodate the changes of mood that
Leone later called for in his Fourth Dialogue. If the stage on which
his comedy was presented lacked the court's sophisticated machinery to
accomplish such effects easily and subtly, these could have been hinted
at. Depending upon the adequacy of the room's ventilation (to let out
smoke and heat from the many open flames of the lighting sources), the
stage could be provided with a modicum of candelabra and oil lamps
to provide the illumination needed to see the performer's features from
perhaps thirty or more feet away, an objective doubtlessly aided by the
actor's wearing a relatively pale makeup to reflect the golden light of
candle- and oil-flame. To enhance the stage's brilliance required for the
comic mood, many of the candles in the wall sconces of the auditorium
could be snuffed out, thereby leaving the chamber in semi-darkness—a
condition prescribed by Leone in his discussion of lighting procedures.
At the première before the Jewish community a similar standard practice of court staging, later recommended by Leone, was followed: that

of placing hoods before each of the stage lamps in the audience's vision to prevent the glare of the flames from shining directly into the audience's eyes. A community that had several decades of experience in lighting court theatre presentations would also know how to use reflectors and tinted glass to intensify the light on the acting area downstage, to utilize special instruments of lesser brilliance for upstage scenery, and to raise and lower instruments placed above the stage to dim and brighten the stage lighting effect.

In contrast to his relatively fully developed descriptions of the technical procedures involved in playwriting and stage investiture, Leone's comments on acting tend to be fragmented and cloudy. Perhaps because in the Dialogues he saw himself as a poet and impresario, he did not overly concern himself with the particulars of the acting craft. During his time, it should be realized, impersonating a role in a play was still not considered high art, in our sense of the term. Furthermore, it was not an occupation of any great social standing, but was viewed as falling between the unskilled laborer and the artisan. As an amateur diversion, however, it was not at all demeaning and was employed to demonstrate the skills of public address and comportment expected not only of the wealthy ruling *élite*, but also of their middle class imitators. Yet something of the attitude towards the professional player (a role which had been forced upon the members of the Mantuan Jewish community) may have colored his thoughts and made him reluctant to treat at length and in detail this significant aspect of performance. As a student of rhetoric (and acting in the Renaissance was subsumed under the rubric of rhetoric), he was certainly aware of the appropriate modes of standing, walking, gesturing and talking on the public platform, and how a speaker, using the figure of *personificatio*, could take on the personality of another human for oratorical effect. What Leone furnishes, however, about these highly technical areas of performance is certain commonplaces (*communes loci*) of rhetoric—basic information and skills that beginning students of the subject acquired as behavior models in their early training. Veridico-Leone, for example, only counsels the actor to use good vocal support and resonance, to speak slowly and articulate his sounds carefully, and to vary his gestures to suit the emotions that were themselves affected by differing stage types. He then furnishes specific instances of the ways in which a comedian playing a miser, a servant, a fool or a maidservant could visibly demonstrate feelings of rage, joy, grief, despair, silliness, sauciness and contempt on occasions when these were warranted. Such bits of business (*lazzi*) were, of course, extensions into comic acting of the commonplaces of visible and vocal deportment suggestive of varying emotional states that the student of rhetoric was expected to master. With Veridico-Leone's brief admonition about the necessity for the speaking actor to accompany his words with equally meaningful action, there is found a similarly brief treatment of the question of whether the actor was to feel his part or simply display the emotions of his role. Leone sidesteps the issue by declaring that both were present if the actor possessed natural talent.[25]

Do these tantalizingly simple and even perfunctory comments of Leone reflect the attitude of his century toward a lower class activity? Or do they mirror, as Schirmann seems to think, the inferior performing skills present in at least some of the cast of the court performances? If the latter were the case, did Leone then have to depend largely on the literary quality of his script and the artistry of the scenery, costuming and lighting to compensate? Or may we infer from the fact that he lauded accomplished professional actors[26] that their art was essentially a mysterious one, that an actor needed only a "natural disposition," and that when such a person learned his part well he naturally found movements and gestures to make himself look real to an audience?[27] Or was Leone deliberately withholding information about performance because he saw it as a complex and esoteric craft that could not readily be imparted to outsiders?

Perhaps some answers to these puzzling questions may be put forward that may also be useful in our reconstruction of Leone's Hebrew comedy performance. We may begin by noting that Leone placed a high regard on the work of the actor. He insisted that if a choice had to be made between an inferior play with good actors and a fine play with poor actors, the preference should be for the former.[28] It is likely that the premium that Leone placed upon acting excellence as a key to a successful dramatic presentation came as a result of hard-won experience. Numerous court performances must have taught the Jewish community and its director that while all players were not of equal ability, discipline in the fundamental techniques of platform deportment could compensate in great measure for less natural skill and so make for a generally effective presentation. Therefore it is likely that the members who were regularly employed as players in the court's performances were well-schooled in what Leone elsewhere terms "corporeal eloquence," and "the movements of the head, countenance, eyes, hands and body."[29] While it is not our place here to provide a complete description of sixteenth-century acting method and manner, some brief idea of normative playing behavior of the time may help to clarify Leone's comments in the *Dialogues* and to suggest the style used in his Purim comedy.

The necessity of being seen under candlelight from the back of a fair-sized room and of being heard in a space of at best moderate acoustical properties was a major reason for the use of a presentational acting style. Actors faced more or less directly towards their audience so that their facial expressions could be seen and their voices heard easily and effortlessly by an audience. So as to address audiences to one side or another of the auditorium while at the same time to seem to talk to their fellow actors on stage, they learned to stand with their feet turned out at approximately a thirty-degree angle, with the heel of one foot directed toward the instep of the other. Simultaneously they stood in a *contra-posto* attitude, achieved by placing slightly more weight on one foot than the other while thrusting the hip of the weighted foot slightly out and forward and counter-rotating the opposite shoulder slightly back and down. The turn-out of foot and gracefully twisting stance were in themselves symbolic of the poised cavalier and lady of quality. The position was regularly used offstage by the ruling classes, practiced by orators and put into their representations of noble and heroic figures by painters and sculptors.[30] We may presume, therefore, that this posture was taken by the upper class characters Amon, Deborah and Ephron, Jedidiah and Asael, at least before they begin to lose their composure under the circumstances of the plot, and by Wisdom and the venerable Rabbi Amitai whose poise reveals their authority. When, however, the first set of characters become agitated they adopt a posture that resembles the comportment of their servants. The most extreme menial stance is affected by the oafish Shovel, although Obed, Pash-hur and Jekarah have this body-set. It was marked by the feet being perhaps a foot apart and parallel to each other, the hips and shoulders in the same plane and the knees slightly bent and the body tipped slightly forward with the shoulders rounded.

To be seen more readily against the darker scenic background, gestures were made somewhat away from the body; with the elbows away from the rib-cage gestures could be larger. Ordinarily it was considered unseemly for persons of good breeding to gesture above the shoulders or below the hips, although when impelled by strong emotion it was acceptable (as does Beruriah in extending her hand heavenward in III, 1). The rhetorical principles for posture also had their symbolic

correspondence in gesticulation. The theory underlying its utilization
(common to the painter as well as the actor) was that inner states of
mind were manifest on the body's surface and in the sounds of speech.
This external appearance could be learned and was reproducible by recalling the original visual and vocal image of the mental state. As part
of his early training, therefore, the student orator, actor (or painter)
had to memorize a repertory of bodily postures, gestures, facial expressions and qualities of voice and articulation identifiable with the
major aspects of thought and feeling. Once well learned and practiced,
these images could be brought to mind and in turn used to produce
concurrently the external attitude and a stir of feeling associated with
the original stimulus. From this repertory of elemental expressions, the
advanced actor learned how to "invent" his own by compounding them
in accordance with the nature of the character he was playing and the
circumstances of the play.[31]

In effect, the rhetorical manner of acting of the sixteenth century required the actor to produce distinctive, recognizable figures of
speech of the playwright's dialogue. Characterization was achieved
when the actor recalled in their proper sequence the states of mind
experienced by the character that the actor had previously memorized
with the dialogue. By and large the technique of recalling previously
learned images produced an emotional response in the actor of a particularly low key, but, on occasion, the actor could generate a higher
level of emotional response by the technique of *personificatio*, or iden-
tifying strongly with his role for the brief moment that he was expected
to project strong emotion to his audience. Such a moment doubtless
occurred in Jekarah's touching soliloquy of Act V, Scene 5. But certainly the technique of the emotional identification was not sustained
or maintained with such depth as is practiced now by Method actors in
naturalistic drama. Although the conventionalized deportment of the
stage actor was based upon the mannered (or unmannered) behavior
of the three social classes, the fact that the actor had to reshape this
behavior into a poetic mold gave a highly theatricalized cast to his
performance. Particularly for comedy, speech and body-action were
informed with the rhythm supplied as a figurative element by the playwright himself, with the movements of the body, by turns gracefully
fluent and expressively posed, counterparted by a voice that, like a
musical instrument, could vary from the smoothest *sostenuto* to the
sharpest *staccato*. The work of the actor possessed in greater part than
it does today the quality of the singer, the dancer and the pantomimist.

We are on safe ground in assuming that Jewish players who had won the plaudits of the court for their acting style would bring something of that achievement to their local Purim celebration. The same production committee entrusted with the responsibility for court presentations[32] may well have been in charge of mounting *A Comedy of Betrothal*. Although no direct evidence can be brought to bear to establish this event, we may reconstruct the production sequence.

It is highly likely that an experienced committee head would decide to initiate the preparations well in advance of the Purim holiday. In this way he could ensure adequate time for the actors' parts to be copied out (each actor did not have the entire play but only his speeches and their cues—his "sides"), to cast and to rehearse the production, and to build and paint its scenery and assemble its costumes. Although when performing at court non-Jews often shared the stage with Jewish actors, it is fairly certain that the Purim celebration made use of exclusively Jewish talent.

Casting was considered an important aspect of the production process; to judge from Leone's words, the success of the play depended in so small measure upon the selection of a fit actor. As has been earlier suggested, a conventional typology of characters was used in the casting process, and we are safe in assuming that there existed within the Jewish community actors who were proficient in performing the patresfamilias, the unworldly lovers, the sly and ingenuous servants and other types which informed *A Comedy of Betrothal* no less than other plays of the same genre.

But we are on slippery ground if we assume the women had a place in the cast. We know that after mid-century women were found among the members of the professional troupes of the *commedia dell' arte* and that some of them performed at the Mantuan court perhaps with Jewish actors. (Leone mentions the name of one Flaminia as having exceptional stage ability.)[33] But evidence and argument point to the filling of female roles with male actors for the Purim play. Even at court, for satiric effect, female impersonators played older women (such as Jekarah) or eccentric upper class wives (such as Deborah). Sometimes at the court theatre as well, older boys or youths who were skilled at impersonating young unmarried women played the *inamorata* parts (such as Beruriah). Hence it was not only an accustomed practice for the Jewish community, but one which could make for efficiency in role selection, since such types of performers were ready at hand.

But, it may be asked, did not trans-sexual casting constitute trans-

vestitism against which Deuteronomy 22:5 specifically warns? Admit-
tedly so, but this was a religious offence that could be offset in several
ways. For one, it was also condemned by the Gentile community for
spiritual reasons, yet condoned for the theatre with the reason being
advanced that it was considered more modest for men to show themselves off as women on stage than for women to play their own sex
before an audience. This was especially the case when the Jewish
community was levied to perform at court, since not to have done so
would have jeopardized the safety of the community. Under such circumstances the leaders of the community would consider it less sinful
for a man to dress as a woman than to place the virtue of modest Jewish
women at risk by setting them on stage to be ogled at by a court where
sexual license was more the rule than the exception. Another reason
may be advanced for justifying the practice of trans-sexual casting and
transvestitism. Purim was a time of carnival when even such a liberty
was tolerated—at least for that moment. It is notable that in the in-
terests of "verisimilitude" playwrights regularly reduced the number of
female roles to a minimum and minimized scenes of intimacy between
the sexes. The fact is only explainable if we recognize that female roles
were ordinarily taken by men. Indeed if a scene of sexual innuendo
were to be made ridiculous, this could be accomplished handily if the
audience recognized the man beneath the female guise (as probably
occurred in Act I, Scene 4 between Jekarah and Pash-hur).

Another reason may be advanced for the general practice of trans-
sexual casting during the Renaissance period—the notion of acting as
a figurative process whereby the *persona* and the actor beneath the
mask were both to be evident to the audience. In this regard Leone's
remark about characterization is pertinent: it was a process intended
to transform but not to transfigure the actor. We may understand this
to mean that the actor was to change his outer appearance, yet not to
the extent that his own personality disappeared beneath the role he was
portraying. Characterization, therefore, was to be on a double playing
level, another aspect of the literal-figurative mode of poetic creativity
of the time and one perhaps most clearly projected by trans-sexual
role-playing. Hence the disguising ploys so frequent in the plotting
of playwrights from Ariosto to Shakespeare, in whose scenes males
played females pretending to be males!

But let us return to the reconstruction of the production sequence.
Once the play was suitably cast from among the men of the community,
the parts were distributed. Thereupon followed a first reading whereby

all could hear for the first time the play in its entirety. In this way the actors became familiar with the nature of the events and other personages of the drama with which their characters were involved. At this first reading, no doubt, Leone as the author was present to furnish his interpretation of the roles to the players, and so to serve, in effect, as an artistic director. Thereafter the actors were probably left alone for several weeks to learn their parts, a relatively short time span considering that they were gainfully employed at other business than the theatre. No more than this time was likely required because of the efficiency of the impersonation process and the experience and skill of the actors. Role-study, as we have mentioned earlier, merely consisted of assigning the proper sequence of expressions required of their characters from moment to moment as set out by the playwright, drawn from a previously memorized repertory of behavior and modified by their personal inventiveness according to the circumstances of the play. Because most of the actors had played together many times before and knew each other's stage manner, the number of "stand-up" rehearsals did not have to be many. An established protocol of "taking and yielding stage"—that is, for capturing and relinquishing the audience's attention, and of entering and existing, and sharing a scene with a fellow player—was well known to all. All that Leone had to do, in all likelihood, as director at these rehearsals, was to assign the exact places and times for entrances and exits and establish the traffic patterns when several characters were moving about the stage, detail the particular "business" expected of the character and judge the stageworthiness of the *lazzi* and actions already supplied by the performance for their characters.

During the interval between the selection of the play and the final rehearsal, in all probability two other kinds of production activities were set in motion. Hitherto the committee charged with the responsibility for presenting the Purim play had solicited funds for its support from the Jewish community. Now these monetary gifts were expended for the design, building and painting of the scenic pieces, and for the acquisition of stage dress by construction, purchase or loan (possibly from the actors' or the court's theatrical wardrobe). The committee also made arrangements for the presentation of intermediary entertainment that it and the director (Leone) had selected to be performed between the scenes and acts to enliven the dramatic event. We may suppose that by the time of the final rehearsal, scenery, properties, illuminating sources and costume were in place for the play and the intermediary entertainments. It is problematic, however, whether the final "run-through" included the rehearsal of the various *intermezzi*. (Earlier these performances by singers, dancers and musicians were prepared quite independently of the dramatic play.) Because of the great length of time (four or five hours) that would be required to run the entire show in the last rehearsal before performance, we may suppose that the intermediary entertainment was reviewed separately, with the performers only being given the cues when they would be on stage at the première performance. The actual running of the show on Purim eve was likely entrusted to a stage manager, a customary office in Italian theatrical presentation, and it was he, therefore, together with his assistants, who made sure that the entire program of dramatic and intermediary material fitted together.

What was the makeup and behavior of the audience that attended the performance? Mention already has been made of the carnival-like character of the Purim holiday, a time when Jews were expected to make merry—even to drink sufficient wine so that they could not distinguish the name of virtuous Mordecai from the wicked Haman. It is likely, therefore, that the community gathered in high spirits to see the play following the evening reading of the Book of Esther (*Megillath Esther*) in the synagogue. In the spirit of the holiday, the audience noisily awaited the start of the entertainment, signaled by the lighting of the lamps that illuminated the stage and the snuffing of the candles in the sconces that lined the walls of the the audience chamber. When this operation had been concluded, an orchestra located on one side of the room or behind the scene struck up a festive tune by way of overture. (We may suppose that the musicians themselves were part of the ensemble from the community that regularly performed for the Mantuan court, and so were quite accomplished in their art.) Finally, on a cue from the stage manager, Wisdom appeared, perhaps walking from the back of the hall or from the wings to the center of the stage to the flourish of trumpets (as Leone himself suggests). Having spoken her prologue, she disappears into the wings only to be swiftly replaced by Amon and Deborah who appear from within the doorway of their home.

Although it was not customary practice to include *intermezzi* in the text (as also scenic locations and stage directions), these were certainly present, offering entertainment on themes related to the holiday and the play. As visual treats for the eye and ear the *intermezzi* must have helped to divert those in the audience who were not able to understand the Hebrew of the dialogue. It is quite possible—again reasoning from the practice followed at other theatres when Latin drama was performed for a general audience, some of whose members did not know the language—that brief synopses of the plot in Italian were distributed as part of a souvenir program. But this again is conjecture and we have no surviving record that this occurred. We may recognize, however, that even for those who were not fluent in spoken Hebrew, the conventional, easily understandable language of facial expression, gesticulation and vocal tone employed by the actor to convey his character's ideas and feelings, projected vividly a sense of what he was saying. If the nice linguistic nuances and verbal jests of the Hebrew dialogue were perceivable only to the *literati*, the entire community could enjoy the skillful slapstick and pantomimic by-play of these "professional" amateurs. Knowing the centrality of the Hebrew language to Italian Jewish culture at this time, we may assume that the segment of non-Hebrew speakers did not disapprove of its presence. For it reminded them of a past (which would in G-d's good time come again) when they were free men and their land of Israel was sovereign. They, no doubt, also welcomed the Hebrew because it was fashionable, the counterpart of what their cultivated Gentile neighbors were doing in reviving the Latin tongue of their Roman ancestors.

The première performance, with the inclusion of the intermediary material as supplement to the dramatic core of the performance, probably lasted until well past midnight. Perhaps then, following the custom of their Mantuan neighbors, the members of the audience separated into smaller groups to attend the numerous banquets laid for them in their private homes, to share with friends the special Haman-tarts and to continue the celebration of the Purim holiday into the small hours of the morning.

Alfred S. Golding

NOTES

1 Pioneer work in the scholarly reconstruction of the life and work of Leone
   de' Sommi Hebreo de Portaleone was begun in the late nineteenth century
   with the publication of L. Carnevali's history of the Mantuan ghetto, *Il
   Ghetto di Mantua*, 1884, and A. d'Ancona's *Origini del teatro italiano*,
   particularly Vol. II of the second edition (1893). In 1898, in *MGWJ*,
   M. Steinschneider had provided a brief history of the man (pp. 467–72
   of Vol. II), and in the same year D. Kaufmann published in English,
   "Leone de' Somi Portaleone (1527–1592), Dramatist and Founder of a
   Synagogue at Mantua," in the *JQR*, Vol. X. These, with other studies by
   Italian and German scholars of the very early twentieth century, provided
   either casual or fragmented information about the man as Jew, poet, and
   playwright. More recently Cecil Roth in his *The Jews in the Renaissance*
   (1959) and Allardyce Nicoll in *The Development of the Theatre*, particularly with the 1966 edition, attempted to provide a more cohesive picture.
   Roth in his book devoted Chapter XI to the Italian-Jewish theatre, much
   of which necessarily deals with the contribution of Mantua and Leone de'
   Sommi. In contrast to Roth's emphasis on the social and cultural, Nicoll
   stressed the theatrical aspect of Leone's activities and was, apparently,
   the first to translate his *Quattro Dialoghi in Materia di rappresentazione
   sceniche* ("Four Dialogues on the Art of Staging Plays") in the Appendix.
   Both, however, have made use of earlier research, particularly that performed as part of a doctoral study undertaken by J. Hayyim Schirmann
   in Germany, and subsequently as a Professor at the Hebrew University
   in Jerusalem. Schirmann was also the academic progenitor of a line of
   scholars who wrote on Leone principally in Hebrew. As a consequence
   of these early efforts Italian scholarship has become very active in the
   area of Italian-Jewish theatrical study and in restoring luster to Leone,
   most noticeably in the reprinting of *Le Tre Sorelle* ("The Three Sisters"),
   one of his surviving Italian plays, in 1969, and in 1970 of the *Quattro
   Dialoghi*. . . .

   Two of Schirmann's articles were significant in resurrecting Leone
   as the author of the first Hebrew play and the founder of a Jewish theatre:
   MTWJ LXXV (1931), 97–118, and "Juda Sommo fondateur du théâtre
   hebreu" in *RPJ* No. 5 (1950), 86–104. Substantial components of the
   first article, particularly, provided the basis for Schirmann's reconstruction of the play from several manuscripts, and are digested in the Hebrew
   Foreword to the published edition of the play in its original language (Tel
   Aviv: D'vir, 1961).

   While earlier investigators (such as P. Perreau in his "Intorno ai dialoghi di Leone de' Sommi," *Vessillo Israelitico* XXI (1883) 373–77 had
   called attention to the existence of the *Dialogues*, it was Allardyce Nicoll
   who gave it prominence as a source of information on Renaissance stag-

ing technique. He did so by liberally quoting sections from it in earlier editions of *The Development of the Theatre*, and with the sixth edition, by providing the entire treatise in both the Italian original and English translation, together with a pithy account of Leone's career.

2 For a history of Manuta's Jewish community in the sixteenth century, Cecil Roth's *The Jews in the Renaissance*, previously cited, has passing references, although Carnevali's work, also mentioned above, is still definitive. Readers of Hebrew may wish to consult S. Simonsohn's *Toledoth HaYehudim B' Dukhasut Mantova* ("History of the Jews in the Duchy of Mantua"), published in 1980.

3 In "Juda Sommo fondateur du théatre hebreu," *op. cit.*

4 For a discussionn of Italian Jewish theatre history in the late Middle Ages and the Renaissance, see Roth, 245–53.

5 Schirmann, Foreword to the Hebrew edition of *A Comedy of Betrothal*, 16.

6 There is scholarly disagreement as to Leone's birth date. It may have been as early as 1525.

7 In d'Ancona, II, 424.

8 There is some evidence that he died in 1586, but there are more substantial grounds to believe this occurred in 1592.

9 For a discussion of the use of Hebrew as a spoken language by Italian Jewry during the Renaissance, see Roth, 308–10.

10 I have summarized these arguments from Schirmann's three major publications: his two scholarly articles and his Foreward, cited above in Endnote 1.

11 So, too, is the metaphoric evidence he adduces to justify the Jewish origin of the theatre: the division into five acts that parallels the five books of the Pentateuch; and even the word *scaena* of the Latin as deriving ultimately not from the Greek *skene* but from the word for street or neighborhood of the Hebrew (*Shikunah*)!

12 Schirmann confirms this attitude in his Foreword, 17.

13 As set out in Leone's Second Dialogue, See Nicoll, *op. cit.*, 263.

14 Here I shall discuss only the dramatic quality of the dialogue, which is recognizable even through the veil of translation, and leave the treatment of the richly allusive Hebrew text to Professor Ahroni, included as a second part of this Introduction.

15 I have deliberately refrained from employing the term "ghetto" to designate the Jewish area of Mantua. Mantuan Jewry for the most part did not suffer under its constraints during the sixteenth century. Indeed many seem to have followed the example of their Tuscan co-religionists by building country houses to which they repaired during the heat of the summer. Only in 1612 were its Jews required to live within the precincts of the ghetto. Roth, 13, 29, 268.

16 Schirmann, Foreword, 22.

17 In this regard Heinz Kindermann sees Leone's *Dialogues* as a summary of typical sixteenth-century staging practice. In *Theatergeschichte Europas* (1959), II, 134.

18 For a fuller history and description of this phenomenon see my *Classicistic Acting* (1984), particularly Chapter III, "Classicistic Imitation and Rhetoric," 71–6.

19 Roth, 258.

20 The practice is still evident in the symbolic importance still given to the *dexter* position in flag etiquette and in formal diplomatic placement (as at ceremonies and banquet-seating). It also survives in the remnants of nineteenth-century stage protocol in present-day acting convention. In this regard see Alexander Dean, *Fundamentals of Play Directing* (1941) 132–3 and 212. The importance of handedness in gesturing is evident in early works on rhetoric such as Louis Crésol's *Vacationes autumnales sive de Perfecta Oratoris Actione et Pronuntiatione Libri Tres* (1620) in which the right hand is favored for positive gesticulation. For a digest of the symbolic nature of handedness in the late sixteenth century, see my chapter entitled "Nature as Symbolic Behavior: Louis Crésol's *Autumn Vacations* and Early Baroque Acting Technique" in *Renaissance and Reformation: The Language of Gesture in the Renaissance*, edited by Kenneth R. Bartlett, Konrad Eisenbichler and Philip Sohm (1986), Vol. X, No. 1 of the New Series, 147–57.

21 A structure similar to the threefold is suggested in the familiar *Adelphi* scene of the Lyons Terence of 1493, although the structure is built of five pieces to represent five distinct houses. A configuration containing two side houses and a center pavilion is found in a similar illustration for *Andria* I, 1 in the Venetian Terence of 1561. These may be found reproduced in Kindermann, *op.cit.* II, 83,85.

22 Indeed, in his *Dialogues* of later date Leone saw value in providing lower class characters with attractive clothing and merely wished to dress his upper class figures in garments of greater richness. In this fashion masters as well as servants would be theatrically more appealing. In Nicoll, 269.

23 Thus Shakespeare's characters in *A Comedy of Errors* were clothed in the Elizabethan fashion, despite the fact that they were supposed to be in ancient Ephesus!

24 What conclusions may we draw from Leone's comments about theatrical costuming, apparent in his Third Dialogue, probably written at least a decade after the première of his Hebrew comedy? We may conjecture that while Leone was relatively inexperienced in practical production matters, by 1550 the Jewish comunity already had performed for more than two decades before the court. It is likely, then, that he acquired their information and used it as a base on which to form his own judgement in the-

atrical staging and particularly in costuming. To some degree, therefore, his Third Dialogue statements on stage dress reflect earlier community practice, as well as his own later experience at Mantua and elsewhere.

25 Nicoll, 226–9.

26 These included a "wonderful Montefalco, a piquant Olivio, a sharp Zeppino of Mantua, and a Zappino of Gazzolo." But these are of apparent lesser fame than the "Flaminia of Rome" whom he mentions as being able to give the impression that she was actually involved in the events of the stage, although young and inexperienced. Flaminia visited Mantua in 1567, but had earlier created a reputation as an actress and may well have been seen by Leone prior to her Manutan performance. Nicoll, 252.

27 Nicoll, 268.

28 *Ibid.*, 266.

29 *Ibid.*, 268.

30 These basic postures were employed down to the early nineteenth century, if we may trust the iconographic and verbal records of that time.

31 For a more complete and detailed treatment of the origins and development of classicistic acting deportment and characterization, see my *Classicistic Acting*, 75–112.

32 As described in Roth, 252, the special committee was appointed by the head of the Jewish community, the *Massaro*.

33 Nicoll, 252.

The Play and Its Poetics

The comedy, *Tsahut B'dihuta D'Kiddushin*, (*A Comedy of Betrothal*), is, as might be expected, modelled in form, structure and composition after the Renaissance comedy, and its characters are reflective of the stock figures of the Commedia dell'arte. However, its language, plot and the essential traits of its protagonists are characteristically and unmistakably Hebrew. It is for this reason that the author of this comedy is rightly considered to be the forerunner of Hebrew drama, for he provides us with the first extant dramatic work of some literary magnitude ever written in Hebrew.

The central plot of the comedy is based on purely Jewish midrash (Tanhuma, Lekh Lekha, 8; see also Gittin 8b and 9a of the Talmud). This midrash, which has a legal thrust, relates the story of a wealthy man who, realizing that he was about to die while far away from his son, bequeathed all his possessions to his slave, allowing his son to choose only one single item from the entire estate. The wise father, mindful of the halakhic law that states that whatever property a slave acquires belongs to his master along with the slave himself, assumed that his son would choose the slave, and that the slave would, in the meantime, meticulously guard his new possessions.

The author of our comedy skilfully utilizes this midrash and its legal implications. In fact, this parable serves as a basic plot thread which laces together the disparate and virtually disjunctive episodes of the comedy and so provides a frame for a web of complex interrelationships.

It is noteworthy that de' Sommi wrote this comedy in an atmosphere that was hostile to the drama, for in the sixteenth century in Italy the theatre was still considered alien to the Jewish spirit and culture. Some three centuries earlier Maimonides, who had viewed the Hebrew language as a sacred and exalted tongue, warned against its utilization for writings that tend to "arouse the power of lust, by praising it and by causing the soul to rejoice in it," because such activities stimulate a base attitude (*Commentary to Mishnah Aboth*). The fact that contemporary Italian and other comedies were generally replete with lewd jests, indecent witticisms and moral laxity, strengthened the hands of those rabbis who were opposed to the theatre in general, and to comedy in particular. It should be stressed, however, that *A Comedy of Betrothal*, although pervaded by a secular spirit, exhibits remarkable restraint in matters of passion and lust and is almost entirely purged of the gross sensuality so characteristic of most of Renaissance drama.

As indicated in its Prologue, de' Sommi's *comedy* has a strong didactic thrust. It conveys the critical attitude of its author towards what he views as deeply rooted social and religious ills current within his own Jewish community. Chief among these "disabilities" are those customs pertaining to betrothal and marriage. Indeed, the bizarre title of the play, which constitutes a strange syntactic, almost unintelligible collocation of words that may be rendered "An Eloquence of Marriage-Farce," already indicates the author's sarcastic attitude towards this Jewish institution as it was practiced by Leone's fellow men. In his view, betrothals are conducted not purely "for the sake of Heaven," but for greed. "Money," as Obed says, "commands all." Women are generally the prime victims of this greed. Thus, for example, Beruriah bitterly bewails her fate: "What shall I do? My father and my mother took me away from my beloved Jedidiah and gave me to a man whom I do not know and can't stand. Has anyone, anywhere suffered so much misfortune? While still young and innocent, women are thrown at men who are total strangers, while men can pick and choose whomever they like for their wives." It should be noted that Beruriah's parents decided to rescind their daughter's betrothal to Jedidiah after hearing that his father Sholom bequeathed all his estate to Shovel, his slave. Deborah, her mother, hypocritically quotes the rabbinical maxim: "The pauper is as good as dead" (translated in the text of the play as: "without [money] life can be pretty deadly.") The strong didactic thrust also finds expression in other aspects of the action: Wickedness is castigated, hypocrisy is ridiculed, justice and innocence are exalted. As such, the comedy provides a fascinating insight into the life of a sixteenth-century Italian-Jewish community. It should not be understood, therefore, apart from the social matrix in which it is embedded.

Another major objective of this play is the demonstration of the linguistic and literary power of the Hebrew language, a goal that served as a strong motivating force for many medieval writers (Seadiah Gaon, Ibn Gabirol, Halevi, Al-Harizi and others). De' Sommi displays a consummate mastery of Hebrew. He constantly draws upon the diverse strata of Hebrew sources (Bible, Mishnah, Talmud, etc.), skilfully fusing whole, or fragments of, familiar verses into an elastic, flexible and vivid fabric. Images and turns of thought are conjured up to provide a multiplicity of connotations. The author seems to toy with the sources: verses are at times plucked from their context, twisted and made ludicrous, stretched and contracted to fit his characters and his wit. Thus, for example, a combination of different biblical phrases provides an apt characterization of the role which greed plays in the author's Jewish community. Addressing Jewish women, Obed says:[1] "Oh you daughters of Israel, bewail this disaster (2 Sam 1:24); even if Hamor . . . desires you (see Genesis 35), you shall readily crouch under him between the sheepfolds (Genesis 49:14), were he to put ornaments of gold upon your apparel (2 Sam 1:24).

Linguistic feats, such as the manipulation and exploitation of sound quality, alliteration and paranomasia abound throughout the play. Here are a few examples: *Amon velo emun bo . . . leshaqer beaemunato"; leda, lehodia, wulhiwada; Efron, ki afrot zahav lo; ve'ekh eskal ubitti eshkal.* Among the remarkable artistic devices employed in the play is the use of *double entendre* and innuendos, accomplished through the cryptic use of allusions and circumlocutions: Such, for example, is a dialogue between two slaves, the man Pash-hur and the woman Jekarah, reminiscent of verses from the Song of Songs:

PASH-HUR: Am I, my sweet Jekarah, to stand forever at your door?
JEKARAH: So, the door is wide open. Can't you see?
PASH-HUR: Give me entrance to your Garden of Eden.
JEKARAH: That Garden is locked and its fountainhead sealed!
PASH-HUR: Well, don't stop me from unstopping it!

As indicated above, the lovers' cravings throughout the play are not explicitly sexual. They are rather developed in allusion, conveyed through images of subtle formulation, bearing delicate sexual connotations. The names of the protagonists, who are generally stock prototypes rather than individuated characters, provide a glimpse into their intrinsic quality. Thus the name Hamdan (Greedy) given to one of the principal *dramatis personae* typifies his unrestrained lust for money, for the sake of which he is willing to sell even his soul: indeed, as Pash-hur rightly remarks, only gold makes him tick. Master Greedy (in Hebrew, *Rav Hamdan*) is firmly grounded in mundane realities, a caricature of the "wise," pompous, verbose and grotesquely comic. His speech is studded with bombastic Aramaic expressions, rather than those of the plainer Hebrew. Deborah is a stingy women motivated also by greed. She is aptly characterized by Amon, her husband: "She stings and poisons like a viper." Rabbi Amitai, the epitome of truth, as his name suggests, displays the splendor of virtuous living untainted by immoral behavior. Beruriah is the embodiment of passive innocence. Shovel, Sholom's slave, becomes increasingly ridiculous with the sudden enormous wealth that has been "bequeathed" to him by his master. All in all, these figures constitute a portrait gallery of colorful, representative types.

The author, it should be noted, despite his consummate mastery of the Hebrew sources, does not soar to great poetic heights, as did some of his medieval predecessors. Nevertheless, he has considerable creative power and has provided us with a new literary genre—Hebrew comedy. His play remains a specimen of a still evolving art that has survived the ravages of time and whose Hebrew poesy can bring to us the delicate fragrance of a by-gone era.

Reuben Ahroni

NOTES

1 The version employed for English readers has departed from the literal version cited by Professor Ahroni, for the latter could only prove meaningful to a readership that, like Leone's audience, was acutely aware of the subtleties of the text from its own intimate acquaintance with the original Biblical sources. The translator has instead elected to capture the overall dramatic intent rather than the coruscation of literary nuance.

Legal Aspects of the Play

All the major plot elements in de' Sommi's *Comedy of Betrothal* turn on matters of Jewish law (*halakhah*) and custom (*minhag*) that would have been well known to the playwright's intended audience. These need to be spelled out here, together with their literary sources.

1) The Shovel-Jedidiah action, which motivates the entire plot, presupposes the ruling of the Mishnah (third century C.E.), Tractate Peah 3:8, that if someone in writing assigns all his property to his slave but withholds any portion thereof, however small, the slave acquires nothing—not even his freedom—since we reason that the man may have intended thereby to retain for himself precisely this slave, and any property acquired by a slave belongs to his master (cf. Babylonian Talmud [=b.], Gittin 8b–9a, Baba Bathra 149b, and, on the latter point, Qiddushin 23b). The narrative in Midrash Tanḥuma, Lekh Lekha 8, which illustrates this ruling,[1] is the direct literary source of the Shovel action.

2) The double betrothal of Beruriah to Jedidiah and then Asael involves the following legal considerations: technically, Beruriah's betrothal to Jedidiah is not affected by the groom's untimely (and only apparent) impoverishment; the contract remains valid and must be upheld. Amon is aware of this, notwithstanding his wife's importunings (I, i). His action to break off this betrothal is morally improper since the groom has not consented. The second betrothal, to Asael, on the other hand, is not legally valid from the outset because the bride has not given her consent, a requirement of Jewish law (cf. b. Qiddushin, 12b–13a, and Maimonides, *Mishneh Torah, Sefer Nashim, Hilkhot Ishut*, 4:1). Nonetheless, this betrothal has the *appearance* of legality, since the proper legal forms have been observed. Ephron's agent has given to Beruriah an object of value (one of the three modes of betrothal in Jewish law, Mishnah [=M.] Qiddushin 1:1; the others are through a writ and through an act of intercourse). She accepts the gift under the mistaken assumption that it is from Jedidiah. Her dumbstruck silence upon learning the truth is construed by the witnesses as acquiescence to the betrothal (since, in Jewish law, silence ordinarily signifies consent). The law thus appears to have been fulfilled when in fact it has not; this allows the plot to proceed (III, 2).

3) Slippery legal logic also characterizes Master Greedy's advice to Jedidiah, which the latter acts upon (III, 5).[2] Jedidiah resolves to have sexual intercourse with Beruriah while she is in the country, an act of elopement "according to the law of faithful lovers" of Renais-

sance theatre (III, 2), but also one of the three legally recognized modes
of betrothal in Talmudic law (M. Qiddushin 1:1; though no longer customary or encouraged in post-Talmudic times). Further, on the legal
principle that "no man treats his act of intercourse as a mere act of
prostitution" (b. Yebamoth 107a, Ketuboth 73a, Gittin 81b), Jedidiah
thereby intends to compel Beruriah's father to recognize the validity of
the first betrothal which has just been consummated.[3] This is a daring
and desperate act on Jedidiah's part, because society will construe it
instead as an adulterous act of intercourse with, or rape of, a virgin
betrothed to another man, the penalty for which is death. Here the
operative law is Biblical, Deuteronomy 22:23–27: "In the case of a
virgin who is engaged to a man—if a man comes upon her . . . in the
open country, and the man lies with her by force, only the man who lay
with her shall die, but you shall do nothing to the girl. The girl did not
incur the death penalty, for . . . he came upon her in the open; though
the engaged girl cried for help, there was no one to save her." Greedy
will invoke this law to save Beruriah from the death penalty (since,
were it ascertained that she had consented to the intercourse, she, too,
would be liable to death). Jedidah, meanwhile, is to feign ignorance of
the second betrothal, so that his act of intercourse would merely offend
against propriety as premature (since betrothal through intercourse, by
de' Sommi's time, was frowned upon, as was premarital intercourse),
but would not be illegal. However, in the ensuing action, the maidservant Jekarah, bribed by her master, comes upon Jedidiah and Beruriah
in the field and accuses Jedidiah of rape. (Beruriah, though hitherto
silent, now cries out for help and is exempted under the preceding
law from the charge of adultery).[4] The charge of rape subsequent is
dismissed when Rabbi Amitai demonstrates that the betrothal to Asael
was, in fact, legally invalid because deception was practiced and the
bride never consented. Asael in any case rejects the betrothal since he
wishes to marry Shirah; Ephron, too, now cognizant of the improper
circumstances surrounding the betrothal, also rejects it (V, 3). In the
end, Jedidiah is guilty only of impropriety, which can be forgiven because he had been wronged and thus acted out of despair.

4) Specious legal dealings also appear in Ephron's trick to get
back at Master Greedy. In order to secure the return of the gold talents
meant for distribution to the poor that Greedy has withheld as executor of Ephron's deceased brother's estate, Ephron feigns agreement
to Greedy's demand that Asael, Ephron's son, marry Greedy's eldest
daughter. Ephron purposely draws up a marriage contract that dos not

specify which of Greedy's two daughters is betrothed to Asael (II, 3). According to rabbinic law, such a contract is invalid because, without specification of which daughter is betrothed thereby, the betrothal falls on both daughters, which is illegal (two sisters cannot marry the same man). Both women require a writ or divorce from the man before either can marry (b. Qiddushin 5lb; cf. Qiddushin 64b ff.). This is a source of some embarrassment and puts the women at a technical disadvantage. Here, too, Rabbi Amitai will propose an equitable solution so that the innocent children shall not bear the punishment for their father's guilt, in accordance with the principle of individual responsibility articulated by Ezekiel (18: 19–20). He will entreat Asael to annul the betrothal agreement retrospectively so that no writs of divorce are required (V, ll).

As these legal turns indicate, the play's didactic thrust is not confined to protesting the pursuit of wealth as opposed to learning and good character in contracting betrothals, but also points out and decries the ongoing tensions pertaining to the Jewish community's highest ideal, the pursuit of Torah-learning. De' Sommi illustrates how knowledge of the law itself is a two-edged sword which can be used for private gain as well as for public good. The play underscores the rabbinic maxim that Torah-learning must not be used "as a spade with which to dig" for one's own selfish ends (M. Aboth 4:5). Also illustrated are the tensions inherent within the very act of Torah-study: the difficulties of rigorous discipline and the ongoing temptation to slackness. The two pairs of students/disciples, Jedidiah and Asael, on the one hand, and Jair and Joktan, on the other, exemplify diligence and laxity, just as their masters, Rabbi Amitai and Master Greedy, embody the moral-intellectual virtues of the lawyer-scholar and their perversion (I, 3 vs. I, 6: II, 5; IV, 2).

Because de' Sommi's play was written as a Purim entertainment, it also includes *parodies* of Jewish learning and exegesis that, by his time, were part of the prescribed observance of the holiday. In the spirit of the Book of Esther, which abounds in sudden reversals, rabbinic tradition made itself the object of mockery on Purim. Inebriation, at other times frowned upon, is a positive commandment on this day, and "Purim-Torah," a parody of actual rabbinic learning and lore, is bandied about for purposes of amusement.[5] In the badinage between the apprentices Jair and Joktan in IV, 2, de' Sommi introduces some authentic Purim-Torah, modeled after the fourteenth-century Italian parody, *Tractate Purim* (by Qolonymos b. Qolonymos), and other similar writings. The humorous name "Rabbi Balaam ben Bibi" (in the original Hebrew text; here rendered "Rabbi Balaam the son of Rabbi Shik-kor [Drunkard]") is found in *Tractate Purim* and refers both to the pagan soothsayer of Numbers 22ff. and to the act of drinking on Purim (*bibere*; cf. Schirmann, p. 166 *ad* 67, 20–21). Jair's conundrum, which juxtaposes the two scriptural verses Esther 7:10 ("And they hung Haman . . . ") and Exodus 16:35 ('And the children of Israel ate the manna"; in Hebrew, "ate ha-man"), is a parody of rabbinic midrashic exegesis which derives additional narrative details and moral lessons from the juxtaposition of diverse scriptural verses on the basis of shared words or textual peculiarities. Earlier in the same scene, Jair quotes Scripture, but willfully apocopates the prooftext, with mischievously humorous results. Isaiah 2:4 "[Nation shall not lift up sword against nation], and they shall not learn war anymore," is quoted, omitting the final Hebrew word, as "And they shall not learn anymore," thus endorsing a recess from legal studies;[6]

The Purim background figures in this play in yet other, more subtle ways. The structure of the play in general as well as in some plot details represents some of the narrative tropes of the Book of Esther (all of these, to be sure, are also standard tropes of *Commedia dell'arte*. Stunning reversals of character's situations figure heavily in both (epigrammatic of the Esther story for the rabbis, is Esther 9:1, *wenahaphokh hu'*, the "opposite happened"). Other resonances include the following: Deborah's stubborn independence of will with respect to her husband Amon ("I do what I wish," I, i) echoes Vashti's refusal to comply with her husband's wishes (Esther 1;12). Amon's subsequent heeding of his wife's advice (II, iv) parallels the situation of Haman and Zeresh (Esther 6:14). The strutting airs which the servant Shovel assumes (III, 3, IV, 3 and 4) call to mind Haman's boastfulness (Esther 5:11 ff., 6:6 ff.). In both cases, "pride goeth before a fall."[7]

To an audience well-versed in biblical and rabbinic literature and the language of each, de' Sommi's play is a delightful *tour de force* which also has a serious side: it illustrates the ongoing sources of tension in human nature and social life that pose a threat to the norms of the Jewish community. At the same time it vividly exemplifies and strongly upholds those norms.

Richard S. Sarason

NOTES

1 The Tanḥuma story actually contains a variation of the Mishnaic ruling: in the story, the master dies and a single item of the property is retained for his son.

2 Greedy's advice to the beautiful wife of the "Italian gentleman" whose creditors he has supported in court (II, 6) is also slippery: she wishes to retain her dowry against the demands of the creditors. According to Jewish law, a woman receives back her dowry only upon the death of her husband or upon their divorce. Thus, Greedy recommends a secret divorce with the dowry to be entrusted to the woman's relatives. That way, the creditors can have no further claim on it. The husband thereafter can remarry his wife through cohabitation (since "no man intends his act of intercourse to be a mere act of prostitution"). He can dispense with the bride-price (since she is no longer a virgin), and the couple can live off the dowry monies that would be disbursed to them as needed by her relatives. All of this is technically legal, although the secrecy of the divorce would forestall the creditors from pressing their claim and is therefore devious.

3 Cf. also Deuteronomy 22:28–29—"If a man has intercourse with a virgin who is not engaged, he shall pay the father fifty shequels of silver and she shall be his wife. Because he has violated her, he can never have the right to divorce her."

4 Jedidiah, beset additionally by the news of his father's death and the apparent validity of Shovel's inheritance (and as a typical Renaissance *inamorato*), chooses to die and "confesses" to numerous other capital crimes. Master Greedy recognized that these additional "confessions" will bear no weight in a court of Jewish law, since self-accusation is inadmissible according to the principle that "the closest relative a person has is himself, and no one intentionally incriminates himself" (b. Sanhedrin 9b, Yebamoth 25b; the testimony of a close relative is inadmissible in court).

5 See Israel Davidson, *Parody in Jewish Literature* (New York, 1907), and Davidson's essay in Philip Goodman, ed., *The Purim Anthology* (Philadelphia, 1964), pp. 330–56.

6 Schirmann, p. 166, *ad* 67, 6 points out that such playful apocopations of scriptural verses were common at this time and already were employed with much effect by Immanuel of Rome (c. 1261–after 1328) in his *Notebooks*.

7 Jacob Shatzky, "The History of Purim Plays," in Goodman *op. cit.*, p. 365, indicates that this theme characterizes most of the medieval Purim plays known to us.

Beruriah and Jedediah

A COMEDY OF BETROTHAL

(Tsahoth B'dihutha D'Kiddushin)

A prose comedy

Cast of Characters

WISDOM, dressed in splendid apparel
AMON
DEBORAH, his wife
BERURIAH, his daughter
JEDIDIAH, a suitor[1]
PASH-HUR, his servant
JEKARAH, a maidservant
MASTER GREEDY
EPHRON
ASAEL, his son, a suitor
SHOVEL, a former slave
OBED, his servant
BAILIFFS of the Court of Justice
JAIR, apprentice lad
JOKTAN, apprentice lad
The venerable RABBI AMITAI

Prologue

WISDOM appears,
dressed in splendid raiment, with crowns and diadems.[2]

WISDOM: I am a figure whom you regard with disdain. Nevertheless, my fame is known in the gates and my glory fills all the earth. While all the nations speak in my name yet it is evident that you pay me little heed—you see my face but dimly and fail to know who I am, what work I do and what the splendors are of the crown and diadems that I hold in my hands.

I, therefore, desire to come closer and to present myself clearly and openly to you. Should I be reluctant and hesitant in disclosing my greatness to those dear friends who love my name, simply because there are many who do now wish to acknowledge my presence? But perceptive persons recognize that my power is mankind's garland, an adornment to ennoble the mind even in a time of suffering. Then perceive and know that I am Wisdom glorified who appears and disappears from view even when near at hand.

Today I have resolved to reveal my greatness totally, that until today you have not seen, and to honor those who follow me. For this is ever my way: to let man's reward stem from his own actions, and to permit his achievements, whether great or small, to spring from his own talents. In this manner I accredit everyone according to his abilities and accomplishments.

It is true that some worldly men boast publicly of being my supporters, while, to judge by their private follies, they demonstrate the opposite. Such persons do me little credit. Meanwhile, the wisest of men are thought by the crowd to be of little worth because they live and act humbly.

It is for this reason that I appear before you in my full glory— so that you may recognize the fools by the way in which they avoid

my presence, and the wise by my light that shines from them like
the splendor of the firmament. The latter can raise themselves to
the heights and so receive from my hands their crowns of honor.
For it is indeed proper that the wise should reap the glory.

I realize that the wise of many lands (whether of Greece,
Cyprus or Turkey), have taken pride in the way that they employ
language to delight mankind. Their works have been performed
before men of distinction and high degree, and in their words
pleasure and utility are perfectly conjoined. Their eloquence has
been used to crush contemptible men and to elevate those who are
worthy and to bring them honor. Now some playwrights among
the gentiles have looked down upon the Jews because they seem
to lack this literary facility. It is for this reason that I have this
day resolved to show that the Hebrew language is not inferior
in its artistic power. Indeed, what is a crowning glory for other
languages is but the glitter of a shoe-buckle for Hebrew. Hence,
men should not deem it a defect in that language because they
have not seen it cast, ere now, into a pleasing comedy. Rather, it
is because the words that constitute this holy tongue are of most
ancient and wondrous origin, and it has seemed unworthy for such
sacred words to be used solely for human pleasure. But what other
languages can do, the holy language can do better. The very proof
of this statement I shall soon place before your eyes. For, if the
play form is novel for Hebrew, its capacity for creating parables
and proverbs is well-known, and so can make it even more marvelous as a medium for theatrical entertainment.

Dear spectators! Do not give credence to those who contend
that it is improper to use the holy tongue in a profane fashion. If
they were truly wise, they would recognize that our sages of old
employed amusing tales and witty sayings to ethical ends. Likewise, the play that you are about to see is drawn from the legends
of the ancients who spoke in the name of wisdom. Likewise it
exalts the teachings of Israel that instruct men to do right in the
sight of G-d and man. For, I, Wisdom, have placed knowledge
and understanding in your hands.

In fine, I shall aid in creating joy and gladness among you.
And I shall grant you that most precious gift, wisdom, that I received from the Source of all wisdom—the King of Glory. So
shall you rejoice and be glad, now and forever, because of my
gift.

ACT I

SCENE I

AMON and DEBORAH his wife

AMON: Proclaim to the citizens of our city that in joy and gladness we
propose to marry our daughter Beruriah to the handsome Jedidiah,
Sholom's son. Our most sincere and heartfelt expectation is that
the future bridegroom's father, Sholom, will return safely from
Damascus, that we may be able to consummate the marriage of our
children during the Purim holidays and so unite out two families.

DEBORAH: Who is more concerned about all these arrangements than
I? For months all I have been thinking about is how to make sure
that our daughter has the things she needs—the gaily embroidered
linen, the fancy sheeting and pillow slips, the fine hats and cloaks,
the splendid dresses and accessories—in short, that she has the
most complete trousseau of any Jewish girl about to be a bride!

AMON: I should scold you for the extravagant way in which your
women deliberately throw money around. Such an extravagance
has no real purpose except to serve your vanity. It neither helps
nor profits anyone.

DEBORAH: I don't deny, dear husband, that we disagree on the question
of dowers. As I see it, by making a simple but generous gift we
improve the lot of our granddaughters. Now, if I differ from you,
it's a difference that is peculiar to our sex. And if every Jewish
woman thinks like I do, how can you say that dowering the bride
is a foolish idea? Besides, we have no one else but Beruriah to
whom we can leave our worldly goods. Surely it's plain common
sense and perfectly appropriate for in-laws to endow the young
bridegroom with additional property and so make his life easier.

Besides, Jedidiah is a good boy, intelligent and handsome, too. To my mind there is none like him anywhere!

AMON: I took all this into consideration when I recognized how superior he was in virtue to all his fellows. So I was most careful not to interfere with your provision for his welfare, and even praised you roundly for your actions.

DEBORAH: But, I, also, increased the number of Beruriah's wedding presents when I discovered what Jedidiah's situation actually was. Sholom, his father, is a miser and has refused to give his son what he needs for his marriage. So long as Sholom lives he won't provide a stitch of clothing for our daughter. So it seems that we must take it upon ourselves to furnish her with her marriage finery—her fine blouse, the linen pantaloons, the vest and coat, the turban and sash. And, if we want Jedidiah to be decked out as a bridegroom should be on his wedding day, we shall have to have two complete suits of clothing made for him, as well.

AMON: Ah, there you speak no foolishness or false prophecy! Now not only do we incur the heavy expense of clothing him but of providing him with a complete wardrobe for all the years to come. You'll be telling me next that we are under legal obligation to furnish his board for the rest of his life? Oh, woe is me! [*Enter a messenger who hands Amon a letter. Amon reads, then sighs as if in pain.*]

DEBORAH: [*Alarmed*] Why are you sighing like that? Are you in pain?

AMON: Because we're in serious trouble. Listen to this. [*He interrupts himself and moves away from the door of his house, beckoning his wife to come close to him.*] I called you out here so that Beruriah shouldn't hear.

DEBORAH: [*She is now almost beside herself with alarm*] Please stop torturing me. Why do you keep moving away from me? What is this letter that you are reading, as if your heart was crushed and broken? Have you had news about Sholom, our "in-law"?

AMON: Yes I have. This very letter is about Sholom and it brings terrible news! Terrible! It says that Sholom has passed away in Damascus.

DEBORAH: Blessed be the True Judge![3] I am so sorry to hear such awful news. But why do you make things worse by mourning him? Doesn't death come to everyone? Well, you have decided— and properly too—to bring that fine young man, Jedidiah, into our household and, as his guardian, you can help him manage his abundant inheritance. With all of this wealth you can maintain him under your roof in suitable fashion.

AMON: Maintain him in suitable fashion? With what? His father has left a cruel inheritance for his dear son. He has deliberately given it all to strangers!

DEBORAH: What a calamity!

AMON: [*Reading further in the letter*] Oh, oh! Can I believe what I'm reading here? And he such a good, upright person, too!

DEBORAH: What more frightening news have you to tell me? Why are you holding it back from me?

AMON: How can I hold it back, and how can I speak out when I see that my "in-law," Sholom, has taken all the joy out of my life. While they were in Damascus, Sholom willed everything to Shovel his servant.

DEBORAH: Alas, alack-a-day and woe upon us all! Is there no way that we can restore the inheritance to his son Jedidiah and so settle things for our son-in-law?

AMON: Well, this is what Hanamel, my partner in Damascus, wrote me. The authorities there blocked any possibility of Jedidiah ever obtaining his inheritance—even the smallest bit of it! So Hanamel has resolved to say nothing about what happened there until he can send me more information. He has written this in strictest confidence to me alone. So don't you be revealing about what's in the letter—not to Jedidiah, not to his sister Shifrah, who is coming to live with us today, and certainly not to anyone else!

DEBORAH: Thank the good Lord that they haven't yet arrived and that the marriage has not been finalized. There's still the chance that one way or another we can find the happiness for our daughter that she richly deserves.

AMON: But am I not obliged to give her in marriage to Sholom's son Jedidiah, this very week?

DEBORAH: Granted, you gave your solemn promise to Sholom's son. But there isn't the least doubt in my mind now that you are completely absolved of that promise, because his father made a mockery of the agreement with you when he handed over his wealth to a total stranger rather than to his own son.

AMON: Just because Sholom failed to do what was right, does that permit me to break my solemn word? The promises I make, I keep!

DEBORAH: Look. There is no question of solemn promises here. Just don't try to give my daughter to someone or other who is weak and helpless, because she would think it a misfortune and not be happy in such a marriage. Before I would give her to such a man, I would strangle her with my own hands or drown her in the depths of the sea! [*She starts back into the house.*]

AMON: Why are you leaving?

DEBORAH: Because I don't want to waste any more words on the matter! [*Her voice rises into a scream of anguish.*]

AMON: Be quiet, my dear wife, or you'll wake the entire household with your racket! I don't want Beruriah to know about this terrible misfortune.

DEBORAH: Well, then, it won't be any problem for you because I'm resolved to say nothing to her until we can get her another bridegroom. That's the only way we can get out of this distressing situation.

AMON: But why—suddenly, in a twinkling—have you reversed your good opinion of Jedidiah and now consider him your enemy?

DEBORAH: Because from the moment that Sholom changed his will I have hated him intensely. I don't feel sorry for his son, either, because now he's been made a bastard. The only reason I would look at him is to give him the evil eye. [*She makes the gesture.*]

AMON: But what crime did the boy commit?

DEBORAH: What's said is said, and there's nothing that can make me change my mind.

AMON: If that's your opinion of him that's your opinion. But what about my view? Am I already dead? Is that the way you think of me?

DEBORAH: Of course you are alive, dear husband. It's from you that I get my ideas. But I still do as I wish, because I have absolute faith in my judgment to know right from wrong and to do what is right. Really now, how can you deliver your sweet and innocent child over to a miserable wretch who is despised and rejected without a penny to his name? Are you going to endow this poverty-stricken fellow with all your worldly wealth?

AMON: The character that Jedidiah had a few days ago is the character that Jedidiah has today. Isn't he still bright and clever? With the aid of such generous endownments he'll regain the wealth that he had before.

DEBORAH: Quite possibly, husband, but the fact remains he's a lot poorer now than last night!

AMON: How can you compare being bright and clever with money?

DEBORAH: How can you compare a soul with a body?

AMON: A soul gives life. Without it the body is nothing—a nobody!

DEBORAH: Money likewise brings things to life, and without it life can be pretty deadly. To have character only means something is lacking. Just to be bright is dumb, unless one has something in the hand. [*She rubs her first two fingers against the ball of the thumb significantly.*] How can I force my daughter into a life of poverty and make her a laughing stock? That I shall never, never allow. I'm going inside now, but believe me, what I want I'll get!

SCENE II

AMON alone

AMON: At this moment I can't even think straight. I'm upset and my mind is in such a whirl that I haven't any idea what to do. A true woman, my wife Deborah. She is absolutely ecstatic about the value of having gold and silver, and so she stubbornly insists upon getting rid of Jedidiah now that he has no money. But he's still a man of learning and certainly not at fault for what has happened to him. Personally, I would welcome him into the family. After all, I pledged my word to him, and how can I break it? At the same time I'm heartbroken. For how can I watch my own daughter made miserable by marrying such a desperately poor man—a person whom fate has turned against[4] and made into a debtor with all the world against him. I'm between the horns of a dilemma, trapped without an exit, because any attempt to change my wife's stubborn view of things is doomed to failure. Even when I try in the most gentle manner to change her mind, she turns on me like a viper and stops her ears; she only hears what she wants to hear. And if I try to get firm with her, I'm only fooling myself, for then she heaves deep sighs and becomes even more set in her ways. If I'm mad enough to strike her or pull her hair a bit just to bring her to her senses, she acts like a balky cow and curses me with a bellow loud enough to wake the neighborhood.[5] Really and truly, it's not worth my while to get on the wrong side of her. Outside the house I'm pursued by trouble; inside I'm hounded by her nagging and shrieking. So I have no alternative but to follow her capricious wishes, no matter how wrong they are. Who can stand in her way?

SCENE III

PASH-HUR, a servant and JEDIDIAH, a suitor

PASH-HUR: Are you aware, Master, of the countless inquiries about your welfare that the wise Rabbi Amitai, the head of the Law Academy,[6] was making today?

JEDIDIAH: I'm not surprised. No doubt he was checking up on me to find out what I was doing. That's because on the very day that my father left for Damascus, he made Rabbi Amitai my guardian.

PASH-HUR: Let me tell you what he really wants you to do—to crack the books from morning to night and read about the dead. Why, even he would absent himself from the company of such book-worms! D'you call that living? Not to eat a single bite the whole day long and not to rest at night? Just to pour over the books by candlelight and almost never take the air, just to get "wisdom and understanding"?

JEDIDIAH: [*Defending his teacher*] The discipline that made Rabbi Amitai wise continues to keep him diligent in his studies. His mind is like a garden that is well-watered with the understanding of many things. Rabbi Amitai is wiser than any other man alive. Such study is not easy for an old man, either. But if wisdom is to be perfectly maintained, it must be constantly exercised. I know, too, that I am his most serious disciple. Yet I think sometimes that even I haven't the strength to stay all the time in the synagogue soaking up his teaching, no matter how wonderful it is!

PASH-HUR: You're naturally smart and full of ideas. Why suffer to gain knowledge?

JEDIDIAH: A blind man can't appreciate color and an ignoramus like you can't sense the joy of serious study and the reward that comes from discovering new ideas, like uncovering buried treasure. Sensing the true meaning of the Torah gives insight into the very nature of Creation itself.

PASH-HUR: What's the use of wisdom if the wise man cannot fill his stomach with it and if it can't get him a fine, well-paying position? [*Jedidiah is silent. Pash-hur continues*] Now this is the way I see

things. The only true advantage in getting rich—its only real joy—
lies in eating and having a good time. And the only genuine honor
comes from being able to hang around the mansions of the best
people. The real world rests precisely on these three standpoints!

JEDIDIAH: You are stumbling about like a blind man who has lost his
way and strikes out with his stick at anything that he cannot see.

PASH-HUR: Well, if I'm stumbling in the dark, I see many in higher
social positions than yours doing the same thing. You, too, sir,
are dancing about exactly like me, singing the praises of what you
love to do best. For, if a day goes by without your mentioning
Beruriah's virtues, you think the whole world has gone to the
dogs.

JEDIDIAH: Are you still arguing with me, you loafer? Why do you
persist in hiding your deep and lasting affection for me behind
that mask of ridicule? How could I not praise her—she who was
fated to be my portion in this world, a goblet brimming over with
love that revives my very being? How could I not always prove
worthy of her love when I see her perform worthy deeds, and
when I see her sweet nature upon her features? Indeed, all her
actions are but outer manifestations that allow us to perceive, as
upon a theatre stage, the ascending levels of glory of the Most
High—He who with a word brought the world into being. By his
word he created goodness and beauty and incorporated them into
female form. Therefore, I shall bless Him and follow His plan by
being with her and cleaving to her.[7]

PASH-HUR: I've seen many men go astray by thinking the course
they're pursuing is worthwhile when it is worthless. They don't
even realize that they're deceiving themselves. But this is what
you're doing today, my dear Master.

JEDIDIAH: If I've made a mistake, I'll certainly not tell you about it.
But, be that as it may, go ahead and knock on the door. [*Pash-hur
knocks*] It seems like a thousand days have passed since I last saw
her.

PASH-HUR: If one short day seems like a thousand since you last saw
Beruriah, how do you feel about a month of days of not hearing
any news and not receiving a single letter from Sholom, my Master
and your father? Today I simply can't stop thinking about him.
Then, too, the dream that I told you about disturbs me. In my
dream I saw him standing by the mast of a ship that was tossed
about in a terrible storm and was on the point of breaking up. To

save the ship, the captain threw all your father's goods overboard
into the sea. Then your father, as well, sank into the depths. . . .

JEDIDIAH: [*Waving his arms to dismiss such nonsense*] This is what
    happens to a tippler like you—you have nightmares when you're
    in your cups. One drink of mulled wine and you see my father
    dead and in heaven! [*He turns his attention to the door, which
    remains closed.*] Now look at that will you? These deaf servants
    inside the house won't answer the door unless I pound with all
    my might. [*He does so.*]

SCENE IV

JEKARAH, Amon's maidservant, PASH-HUR, JEDIDIAH

JEKARAH: Who's that knocking on my door?

JEDIDIAH: Open up, Jekarah, my darling. [*The door opens*]

JEKARAH: Is that really you Master Jedidiah? You are most welcome,
    because my mistress is absolutely sick with longing for you. [*Je-
    didiah goes inside, Jekarah remains, leaning on the door.*]

PASH-HUR: My sweet Jekarah, am I forever to stand outside in your
    street?[8]

JEKARAH: No, the door is wide open. Can't you see?

PASH-HUR: I shall now enter your Garden of Eden.

JEKARAH: That Garden is locked and its fountainhead sealed.

PASH-HUR: Well, don't stop me from unstopping it.

JEKARAH: Just look at this worthless, shameless fellow! Keep your
    hands off me or I'll poke out your eyes with my distaff and spindle!

PASH-HUR: Would you be so cruel as to poke out the eyes of your slave,
    Pash-hur, without feeling the least bit of pity for him? What did
    I ever do to you? All that I have is yours; you can twiddle me all
    over without my asking, "What are you doing?"

JEKARAH: Such high and mighty talk shows the folly in the fool!

PASH-HUR: [*Embracing her*] I won't let you go until you change your
    curse to a blessing.

JEKARAH: You'll be blessed whenever I can get some peace and quiet.

PASH-HUR: That's not exactly what I had in mind.

JEKARAH: What do you want of me, you barnyard animal?

PASH-HUR: To plant seed and make life grow!

JEKARAH: May your offspring be forever buried inside a thick wall
    and never see light![9] How come you're not ashamed of your own

impudence? Why don't you learn to behave like your master? He's a real prince and a charmer, that Jedidiah of yours. He's an honorable, decent young man, always gentle and soft-spoken with my mistress Beruriah. But no more on that subject, lest anything evil comes to her betrothed [*she spits three times to ward off the evil eye.*] But you—you deceitful and cunning rogue, the monkey-business that he wouldn't do himself, you do for him. I've seen that from the moment I first laid eyes on you.

PASH-HUR: Who else knows me like that and tells me all about my real self but you! [*Jekarah breaks away from his embrace.*] Why are you running from me?

JEKARAH: Because I hear my name being called from inside the house.

SCENE V

MASTER GREEDY, a lawyer and JAIR, his apprentice lad

MASTER GREEDY: I note that this is the door of Nahum of Galilee, swinging about and open to every breeze. The Italian gentleman who is the father of the bride—I told you about him before, the one dressed in a green-colored gown with a black hat upon his head—go and ask him how he is and then come back and tell me. Inform him that I'm here, ready to hear whatever he wishes to tell me. Come back directly with his answer.

JAIR: Yes, sir.

MASTER GREEDY: I really don't know what this Italian wanted from me today when he let me know, by means of a messenger, that I must absolutely promise to meet him to discuss a confidential matter. He wouldn't think me so dishonest as to reverse the opinion that I wrote against him when I acted for the court as referee and decided for his creditors. I understand that now they've all gotten together to demand his property when he couldn't cough up the money. To prevent his creditors from throwing him in jail, he has taken refuge in the house of Nahum, his father-in-law. He doesn't dare show his face outside except at night, at the hour when bats swarm from their hiding place.[10] If this is what he wants me to do—to find for him and not his creditors—why then he's completely out of his mind. For I shall not change my opinion—absolutely not—in this case, although there are a good many ways for me to reverse myself, like a piece of sealing wax, and to support this debtor's

claim. But I wouldn't think of doing it, now that I've moved down
from the Galilee. As I have only recently settled in Sidon, I have
resolved to watch very carefully what I do, so that I may develop
an excellent reputation with the local citizenry. I have, therefore,
been strict with myself about the kind of cases that I take, despite
the fact that I have been deluged constantly with requests for my
legal services, and showered with gifts by prospective clients who
wish me to intercede on their behalf. But here comes the lad from
the house. Did he have a word with the man?

JAIR: [*Breathless from running*] I found him at last in one of the rooms
and spoke to him, as you bade me. He replied that in all sincerity
he wished merely to honor your fine character. He's in the inner
courtyard, waiting to talk to you.

MASTER GREEDY: I shall carefully consider what he has to say. Meanwhile, return to the house and keep yourself busy for the next few
days. I shall be occupied with several important matters, so I can't
teach you about the law business. Don't fool around or you'll be
severely punished.

SCENE VI

JAIR, the apprentice lad alone

JAIR: [*Kissing his finger tips*] May my mother be praised to the skies
for apprenticing me to this law teacher, at whose home I take
my supper. I'm really and truly sorry that she only gives him a
measly thirty pieces of silver a year for my keep. Such money
is nothing compared to the fabulous life I live in his house, and
the tasty meals that I eat at his table, morning, noon and night.
Day in and day out, more and more people bring him presents in
token of their appreciation. There's no end to their giving: dairy
and meat dishes, and fish and eggs right around the clock! I stuff
myself on all sorts of delicious food, and when I've had enough of
one dish I send for another. It's also true that my mistress forces
me to dash back and forth a hundred times a day from the house
to the market on some errand or other, or to carry something for
her—but what of that? Toiling over my books is far greater labor
than doing the kind of work I do. All day long this fine teacher of
mine is engaged in various kinds of business, so he hasn't much
time to devote to teaching me. That way I have lots of time to

fool around with the other apprentices! Just look at these seven pennies I got as a present from Aroodi, and this inkwell from his brother Arali. I couldn't be happier! Really, it's been only a month since my 'prenticeship papers were signed and celebrated with a Temple offering, and to this day my Master hasn't taught me a blessed thing about the law! But who's worrying? Right now I'm on my way to the toy shop to buy another ball to play with. . . . I think this one's worn out!

ACT II

SCENE I

PASH-HUR: May you live and be well, Master. It's really shocking to hear Amon and his wife talking about whoever it is they're complaining about. And then, did you notice how nervous they were when you came in. There wasn't the usual fuss they make over you as the prospective son-in-law. They didn't even bother to hide the angry expression on their faces, and the silence was so heavy you could hear a pin drop. If anything, they became even madder when they saw you.

JEDIDIAH: Is everyone supposed to be deliriously happy all the time? Aren't you supposed to feel sad at hearing disturbing news or when trouble's brewing? Even so—though my sweetheart Beruriah has already freely and formally consented to be my wife—I'm beginning to worry when I see both her parents quarreling like that.

PASH-HUR: That's the very reason I allow myself a drop of beer and a swallow of wine now and then—to keep myself from becoming bad-tempered and to keep trouble from the door. Come on, Master, let's get back to our lodgings, tickle the lute and sound the viol, and have a fine time. Just don't give in to despair and despond, for such thoughts prompt the body to moodiness and melancholy.

JEDIDIAH: A turn about the country is probably the best idea, because he who sings while heartsick only makes himself more miserable.

PASH-HUR: In that case, get out of town and hit the open road! [*They leave*]

SCENE II

AMON and his wife, DEBORAH

AMON: How can I escape from this fix without giving up my view of things and taking over yours—a view that calls evil good and good evil? May the All-Merciful have mercy on me, for as G-d is my witness, I know it's not my fault that I have to refuse so fine and handsome a youngster as husband for our daughter!

DEBORAH: Well, when he was rich he was handsome and fine. But now that he's without wealth he's a disaster. Everybody knows that for a fact. Poverty and penury don't do a bit of good for anyone!

AMON: You speak plain foolishness. Just realize how crazy you are to place a veil over your eyes that blinds you to the truth and prevents you from seeing all the harm you're doing to me by chasing him away, even though he's innocent of any wrongdoing. What do you find so painfully lacking in him that makes you force me to go against my better judgment? I sincerely believe that if I give in to your wishes, a calamity will befall us because G-d observes all our wrongdoings, you know. But what can I do against your obstinacy, arrogance and bad-temper?

DEBORAH: Today I forbid you to vent any more of your spleen against me. From your angry and bitter words I sense that you are sick at heart.

AMON: Why shouldn't I be when I must run after you and gulp your words like water? All who see me will laugh at me and turn away when they learn I broke my word to Jedidiah in not keeping our contract.

DEBORAH: That's just not so, my dear. That's not the way it is at all! If you will only use your head, you'll see that everything will come out right. Because, my dear husband, it's not you who is breaking his word, but Sholom who did injury to his son and damaged the boy's reputation. If you promised to give our daughter Beruriah to his son Jedidiah, well, open your eyes and you'll see that this is not the same Jedidiah, for on his deathbed, Sholom believed him to be a foundling from the marketplace.[11] So, if he's not his true son, then in truth, you should not be his father-in-law.

AMON: Are you trying to make me look foolish by suggesting that our daughter's betrothal contract, that I signed and entered into most solemnly, was not water-tight?

DEBORAH: An agreement like that can be broken as easily as a thread
parts in a flame. Haven't I heard you say often enough that there
are many reputable experts who can remove such an obstacle from
your path and provide you with an opportunity to nullify and void
an agreement, and that this can be done without violating the law?

AMON: [*He puts his hands to his ears*] I'll not listen to your advice!

DEBORAH: Look, there's Master Greedy, our neighbour. I myself
heard you declare him to be unequaled in getting people free from
legal entanglements. You said, yourself, he's a shrewd lawyer, that
he can argue a case from any side, that a man's fortunate to be
Greedy's client.

AMON: Yes, because he knows how to make up lies and get around
whatever stands in his way. But is it the truth and only the truth
that I love. On my soul, I'm extremely distressed that we are
doing such wrong to this poor orphaned youngster. When I spoke
against him, I did it with an honest mind. I was simply going
along with your viewpoint.

DEBORAH: You should be very pleased to accept my view of things,
because much good can come from it in the future. If you were
listening so attentively to what I was saying, you would also know
that today I am sending Beruriah with her attendants to my sister
in the country. She'll stay there for a week or so.

AMON: Why, just now, did you think of this?

DEBORAH: To discourage Jedidiah from coming to our home, as he
did the day before yesterday. Then we'll not have to be the one
to tell him about his misfortune. This we've agreed upon.

AMON: No matter how I protest I can always be sure you'll inveigle
me into doing whatever it is you want. So the best thing for me
to do at this point is to give in. But what are we going to do with
Shifrah, Jedidiah's sister, who has been staying with us? Will you
make her accompany you to the country?

DEBORAH: No, husband, I will have her stay in the house in the care
of old Sarah, who will see to it that Shifrah cannot escape from
her quarters. And while I'm away you should devote some time to
advancing the welfare of your own daughter, as you promised you
would, so that she can make a good marriage. May I remind you
that some three months past I observed Asael, the son of Ephron
from Tekoah, hanging around outside the house and peering into
the windows. I think that he's sincerely interested in Beruriah, and
it would be a good idea to give our daughter to him in marriage.

He's the soul of generosity, he's endowed with good looks, and as you know, though born poor he now has a great deal of money. So, my husband, it's your bounden duty to get yourself over to the house of Ephron, his father, as quickly as possible. Even though he's a very busy man, I know that he'll receive you without delay.

AMON: Well, well, since I've always bowed to your requests in the past, I give you promise that I'll find him and speak with him.

DEBORAH: Don't you see, my husband, that a Power higher than ourselves is telling us that we should extend this invitation to him? I'm quite fond of this boy, and word has it that he's there with his father, right now. So, please, go quickly, husband, and don't dally on the way, for this is important family business and we shouldn't let anything interfere now that there is a chance for things to work out well for us.

SCENE III

EPHRON, ASAEL; later, AMON

EPHRON: Conduct yourself discretely with our friend, the Duke, when you confide the information that sly Master Greedy is withholding from my late brother's estate the talents of gold entrusted to his keeping for the poor of the community. Some time ago I heard that he was putting this money into his own pocket, as if it didn't belong to anyone. He thinks he can get away with it because he's above the law, and that no court can take it away from him. Now he adds insult to injury by suggesting that if I agree to have you marry his daughter, he'll return the gold and be a father to you, exactly as I am. That's what he said! When I heard such gall, such impudence, as if coming from a person who had never heard of the Ten Commandments, I was furious. But angry as I was, I resolved to pay him in the same coin. Quickly I pretended to fall in with his plan—that I wanted you to marry his daughter. But I pretended to do so just to get back at him for making me look like a fool when this whole affair started. For at that time, when I confronted him privately about his holding back the money, he laughed in my face. Now I want all to know—those of high as well as low degree—that as the Good Book says: "Even foxes may be caught in the fowler's snare."[12]

ASAEL: I'm surprised that the lawyer in him did not smell out your
hidden scheme. Hasn't he learned the elementary law that where
there are two eligible sisters, the marriage contract must identify which of them is to be wedded. Otherwise such a marriage
may be dissolved only by the issuance of two separate bills of
divorcement, one for each sister. Presumably he knows this, for
he occasionally attends the lectures of the Law Academy.

EPHRON: But when he's there he's not interested in learning what is
right and just, but how he can get away with illegal actions and
promote suits in the courts. All the while he gives the impression
of being a modest man, solely to disguise the fact that his real
interest is in gaining wealth and power. Nevertheless, his face
betrays his evil intention.[13] He has no respect for the law and no
regard for anybody. Now you must go and procure an audience
with the Duke. In this way I can indict Greedy, though I won't
expose him out of respect for the Duke whom he has befriended.
Once Greedy recognizes what hold my son's marriage contract
has over him, shrewd man that he is, he will speedily return to me
the money for the poor, so that I may distribute it. But let him
act quickly, before I publicly denounce that shyster!

ASAEL: I shall speak of this to the Duke without mincing any words.
Perhaps to protect Greedy from disgrace, he will move quickly
and something good may come of all this.

EPHRON: Well, I trust the Duke completely. Now don't stand around
loitering about the city until dawn, but mount your horse and ride!
Success to your journey!

AMON: [*Entering*] Here's Ephron slowly coming along the street. I'll
follow him at the same pace, and when he gets to the market
square, I'll speak to him.

SCENE IV

ASAEL and JEKARAH, Amon's servant

ASAEL: To whom can I turn in order to let my beloved Shifrah know
that I must leave Sidon? Hello, . . .here's Jekarah, Amon's maid
servant, coming out of his house. [*He addresses her*] Just my luck
to find you here on this lovely day, Jekarah, my darling. First, let
me say that the promise I made to you I'll keep. Accept from me
these five coins and buy yourself an ankle bracelet.

JEKARAH: Thank you kindly, good sir. How can I repay all the favors you have showered on me?

ASAEL: I shall be rewarded enough if today, while you are waiting on Shifrah, you mention my name to her. For she is the light of my life, this lady who presently lives in the house of your master, Amon. Your debt to me is discharged, if only you speak to her about me and bring her my greeting. Tell her that I am commissioned for now to mount and ride some eight miles out of the city, but that I will return this evening. Meanwhile, I shall try to find for her that newly printed poem on the glory of women you told me she wanted to read.[14]

JEKARAH: I'm always at your service. But when I tried to talk about you today, she drove me away. She even refused to hear me speak your name.

ASAEL: What's all this?

JEKARAH: It seems she overheard something about marriage plans between you and Master Greedy's daughter.

ASAEL: Isn't it quite clear to her why we're doing this?

JEKARAH: It's quite clear that you're doing this to humiliate her by pretending that you want to marry her so you can turn your back on her.

ASAEL: G-d forbid that I should do such a thing!. Why, my heart is ever glowing like a furnace for love of her. If I contracted marriage with the daughter of that wicked man, it was only at my father's instigation. We did so to put Master Greedy in a position of public ridicule, so that we could recover the money left in his keeping. Now both his daughters require a bill of divorcement from me because I just betrothed myself to one of them, but did not specifically mention which one. Nevertheless, I absolutely spurn them both!

JEKARAH: If what you tell about this shyster is really and truly so— well, he deserves having the book thrown at him. I'll explain everything to Shifrah, because she's pretty mad at you and this explanation will go a long way to bring her out of the dumps.

ASAEL: Go and tell her the whole truth: that my only desire is to be with her, to live under the same roof with her, and never to part from her, for she is my portion in this world. Tell her that I'll prove it to her with all my heart before this day is out. I must hasten away to carry out this business as planned, but when the moment is right, be sure to let Shifrah know that she is always in my thoughts.

JEKARAH: I am your most obedient servant, my lord, ever ready to do
your slightest wish.

SCENE V

JAIR and JOKTAN, apprentices[15]

JAIR: Why are you rushing off like that?

JOKTAN: Is that you calling, Jair, my friend? Well, I'm off to class
and pressed for time.

JAIR: Do you have to run to get there?

JOKTAN: Must the fox run before the dogs? Obviously, my friend,
if I don't get there before my master at the hour scheduled for
lessons, then woe betide my rear end!

JAIR: Don't get scared! Nothing is going to happen to you. I'll stop
him and delay his arrival.

JOKTAN: Hasn't the third hour of morning passed already?

JAIR: So what if you haven't come by the third hour! Just give me
that piece of sweet carob in your hand and you'll hear good news
that'll make you jump for joy.

JOKTAN: Here, take two! Take four pieces! Take an apple! Now
what's so exciting?

JAIR: The news is that today our Master is not going to teach us
lessons. And in the future as well. Not one chapter! He's supposed to be very busy with two big cases, and he's not expected
home until dark.

JOKTAN: If you're playing a trick on me, you know what I'll do to
you. . . ! [He gets Jair by the collar.]

JAIR: Look. I've just gotten back from walking around, and the news
is all over town! If you're interested now in gambling with me,
here are ten silver coins that I can put up against ten of yours.

JOKTAN: Sorry about that. . . . What kind of a game do we play?

JAIR: Why, with the cards that you always keep in your pocket—the
forty-eight card deck!

JOKTAN: A major unprecendented disaster has struck! I'm heartsick
to have to tell you the bad news. My Uncle Ephron got excited
when he saw me playing with them and tossed the pack into the
fire. So now they're all burned up. He gave me a tremendous

walloping too, with a double strap, until I had no strength left in me.

JAIR: Punishing you like that is really rotten. It's unprecedented and you deserve my sympathy. I have just the game to cheer you up. First we'll eat your carob fruit. Then we'll gather great handfuls of berries and keep count—berry for berry—to see which of us can eat more. Here's an excellent spot by the door for us to play. . . .

JOKTAN: [*Holding his stomach as if anticipating a bellyache*] I don't think it's a good idea to compete to see which of us can eat the most berries. Besides, I'm worried that my uncle will pass by, see me and give me another licking. But I'll tell you what we can do, let's walk on to class even if our troublesome master is not there, and we don't have to open a book. If he returns—well, then, he won't get angry at us, because he'll think that all the time we've been preparing our lessons.

JAIR: That sounds like a good idea to me. Let's go and see what will happen. [*They leave.*]

SCENE VI

MASTER GREEDY, alone

MASTER GREEDY: So, today I wasn't too far off from what I thought I should hear. That Italian gentleman has confided that he has big legal problems and desperately wants me to help him with his creditors. He says that he has many who are suing him for damages, and that he hasn't a thing left in his home. All the while he's telling me this, he's sighing and moaning pitifully. Despite all his pleading I was not persuaded, but became even more resolute, like a soldier before his adversary. However, just as he was on the point of finishing his entreaty, his wife showed up. She was absolutely stunning—beautiful as the full moon—I haven't seen her equal in the entire length of Israel. She also had a marvelously clear way of pleading her cause. She spoke of the hardships that she had endured, setting them off, one by one. Well, the burden of her "speech" was that she wanted to recover her dowry money from her husband's creditors. This, as she put it, would "save her life." It seems that she wasn't able to retrieve what was due her through the courts as long as her husband remained alive. When she raised her voice to bewail her plight, my sympathies were aroused. Well, after all, I was not nursed by an ostrich that abandons its eggs and has a heart of stone—mine is still flesh and blood. And what living, breathing man would not have pity on so exquisite a creature being forced to descend into a life of shame and reproach. Because I am a most compassionate son of a compassionate father, I came swiftly to her aid! I gave her this advice on how to rescue her marriage-money: first they should pretend to separate. Thereafter, I would have a court convene secretly, so that her husband, unbeknownst to his creditors, could privately present her with a bill of divorcement along with the dowry money that then would be entrusted to her relatives. And once that step was taken, how could it be undone? Afterwards, they could marry again without any monetary compensation. The wife, children and husband could then live on the returned dowry, disbursed to them by her relatives as needed, thereby providing the family with the wherewithal to live.

Both the lady and her husband accepted my advice with enthusiasm. Of her own will she pressed twenty pieces of silver into my hand with such vehemence that I hadn't the heart to refuse. So, to please her, I pocketed the money—but with the proviso that it was for distribution to the poor of Galilee. [He assumes a pose of piety, then winks to hint the contrary] In this fashion I assisted an unfortunate couple in getting back on their feet without their suspecting why I did it. [He sees Ephron and Amon returning.] But here comes my friend Ephron. I'll hide and eavesdrop. [He conceals himself close by in an angle of one of the houses.]

SCENE VII

AMON, EPHRON, MASTER GREEDY

AMON: Believe me, Ephron, you are like a brother to me. So I must tell you that I'm convinced that my dear friend Sholom recognized that there was something wrong with his son Jedidiah when he denied him his inheritance. Or else, he must have found out something shameful about his wife that made him think that Jedidiah was illegitimate. Since this seems to be the case, my wife and I agree that we couldn't give him our daughter in marriage.

EPHRON: Really and truly, if there was a hint of suspicion about the background of the poor fellow, no man would think you unreasonable in withholding your chaste daughter from him. In doing this you'd be in total agreement with the deceased father, for in arranging this estrangement he must have known he was ruining his chances for a good marriage.

MASTER GREEDY: [*During the previous speech he has been unable to catch a word, although he has tried his best to do so.*] If I don't go closer, I won't be able to overhear what they are saying. [*He sneaks close to them without being seen.*]

AMON: Since his own father has good cause for rejecting him, I may do so as well. In consequence, I am here to request Asael, your son, for my daughter. He will be like my own son. Although it is contrary to common custom for the father of a marriageable girl to pursue an eligible bachelor, I am doing so. The great affection that has existed between us since our youth causes me to break with this convention. That's why I'm here to see you.

EPHRON: Between two close friends like ourselves there is no need to beat around the bush, so let's come to the point. You have already told me the whole story, so let there be no further talk about presuming on friendship. I wish to have your estimable daughter become the wife of my son. As a sign of my willingness, I raise my hand to Him who dwells on high to ask that He favor us with kindness and endow us with blessing, and say to the union of our two families, "This is good!"

MASTER GREEDY: I am shocked by what I hear. . . .

AMON: [*He also raises his hand*] Agreed, and may He act mercifully with us. In spite of the fact that Asael you son and my future son-in-law will not return from the country until this evening, you may wish to announce our plans to the public today so that everyone will know that I have betrothed my daughter to your son. In this way Jedidiah will hear the news and will not return to my home any more.

EPHRON: I shall do as you wish.

MASTER GREEDY: [*To the audience*] Did you ever hear the like?

AMON: To confirm my proposal absolutely and positively, why don't you send your representative to place a gold chain about the neck of my daughter Beruriah as an engagement present from your son, Asael. In this way the betrothal will be made legal and can be formally acknowledged by all and sundry. Thereby, I shall obtain my objective—to make Jedidiah, of his own free will, break his engagement and no longer bother us.

EPHRON: I shall send an elder of my family immediately to your home, while you announce our plans to the community.

AMON: I'll get back home and await his arrival with impatience.

EPHRON: He'll come as quickly as possible. [*Ephron exits*]

AMON: [*To audience*] Many people say that the advice of a child or a woman—both of whom speak on impulse and without reflection—is prophetic.

MASTER GREEDY: [*Overhearing*] Such an impulse in a woman, a fool, or a child may be prophetic—but they don't know what they are saying!

AMON: [*Continuing his soliloquy*] Who is there like me who can predict what is to be? Today I took my wife's advice and got quick results. I hardly began to speak when Ephron fell in with my plan and I concluded a marriage agreement with him. Since from the start things worked out as I wanted, I can only conclude that all is going well, and nothing but good can come out of all this. Because I have faith in Him and accept what will be, I look forward to a bright and happy future—when I will not be the butt of my wife's anger. [*He exits*]

MASTER GREEDY: I am startled to hear such shocking news! Now I'm terribly disturbed because I originally planned to have Ephron's son become my daughter's husband. Yet I'm certain that Amon doesn't recognize the consequences of what has happened. Otherwise, why should he have offered his only daughter to a man who has another wife?[16] The women would then be a constant source of irritation and trouble to each other. Indeed, what would possess Ephron to have his son take two wives? For my part, I know very well that when Amon hears about the first wedding he will cancel the second and things will be as if nothing happened. So I am not bothered about these matters, because they will fall through of their own accord. One thing more. I wonder why Amon decided to break the first wedding contract, after having long since promised his daughter to Sholom's son, Jedidiah? But here's that very person emerging from the house and looking most sad. Let's step back a bit and catch something of what he's saying.

SCENE VIII

JEDIDIAH the suitor and PASH-HUR, his servant

JEDIDIAH: I am really lost if Amon should do this awful thing that the people entering through the garden gate told me about.

PASH-HUR: Woe is me! Misfortune has undone us! We are as good as dead!

JEDIDIAH: I am wretched. Certainly they must have found me guilty of some crime that I unknowningly committed. I say this because today I saw Deborah's face and it was livid with rage.

PASH-HUR: How could they find you guilty of doing wrong? Who can malign a saint or sully a man of virtue? The stars tell me it is Asael who is behind all this chicanery. He wants Beruriah, your betrothed, for himself and is scheming to blacken your name with Amon and his wife in order to turn them against you. By his smooth talk he has made them your enemy and stolen your sweetheart from you.

MASTER GREEDY: [To audience] Here's a place to get into the action. I'll speak up and make it worth my while.

JEDIDIAH: I don't doubt that Asael has defrauded me of what is rightfully mine, so with the wrath of Heaven I'll pursue him and bring misfortune down upon his head. My hand shall grasp the keen blade of justice and I shall save myself through my own power. I shall seize him who offends me even if he ascends to the very heavens!

MASTER GREEDY: [Coming forward] May He who delivers the despairing confer His mercy upon you!

JEDIDIAH: [Turning about and seeing Master Greedy. He is struck by the note of sympathy in the voice of the latter] Sir, are you not Master Greedy, the well known counsellor-at-law! Please don't think me impolite for not greeting you earlier, but misery and suffering have prevented me from seeing you approach.

MASTER GREEDY: I could not help but note the worried tone in your voice and the tear in your eye. Your trouble grieves me. When I heard of the wrong done to you, I became so agitated that I could restrain myself no longer. Therefore, I'm here to suggest something that may soothe your troubled spirit, and to prescribe a remedy for your misfortune. Clever men have ready ways to avoid the disaster that would otherwise harm decent folk, and they have the means to raise up the downtrodden. Don't be misled into

believing that a weaker person cannot triumph over a stronger
enemy. For there are champions in Israel who can save those
who have been injured from the hands of their oppressors. Why,
then, are you standing like one struck deaf and dumb? Stand up
and fight for your rights!

PASH-HUR: That's the very thing I told him to do!

MASTER GREEDY: "All that your hand finds to do, that you shall do."
For that cause there is no lack of weapons.

JEDIDIAH: Who knows what to do or to whom I should run for help
besides yourself, good sir! Yet if you will indeed help me, I
foresee no reward but retribution for yourself from those who are
my enemies. Therefore, dear sir, please don't bother to try to help
me out of my plight, lest I drag you down with me. For I am like
a man who is drowning.

MASTER GREEDY: [*His face noticeably changes when Jedidiah speaks
of "no reward." Now his attitude is cool and distant.*] I'm sorry
to tell you, but at this time I cannot properly defend you as your
attorney of record in presenting your case before the court.

JEDIDIAH: Why did you, therefore, raise my hopes, only to dash them?

GREEDY: Because I must attend to pressing business. But, of course,
you have no lack of legal counsellors here in the city, the least of
whom is far abler than I to direct you how to proceed in your case.
But let me give you a word of advice. Be sure to reward him most
generously with coin of the realm. [*Here Greedy rubs thumb and
first two figures together and looks significantly at Jedidiah and
Pash-hur.*]

PASH-HUR: [*Aside to audience*] Just look at this shyster slyly demand-
ing a fee for his services!

MASTER GREEDY: [*Continuing*] Don't hesitate to give him one or two
talents. In that way he will certainly comply with your request
and provide a subtle stratagem that will enable you to bring your
case to a successful conclusion.

PASH-HUR: [*Admiringly to audience*] What a marvelous pitch!

JEDIDIAH: I have no one here in the city to take my side and advise me
as to how to proceed except yourself. Moreover, I shall pay you
most handsomely for your services, exactly as you have suggested.

MASTER GREEDY: Heaven forbid that I should be found accepting
money for my legal work! For me, conscientiously rendered service is reward enough; I need no further compensation. From
my earliest days I have always operated in this manner, my boy.

Surely you must have recognized that! I must say, however, that sometimes I have to abstain from the myriad details of an active law practice that involves taking the pain of others upon my own shoulders. Otherwise, I should sink to the ground under the weight of such a burden.

PASH-HUR: [*Aside*] Now he makes himself out to be a noble-hearted fellow!

JEDIDIAH: If you cannot relieve me of this great load, I know surely that I shall fall down and rise no more. And, if I will disappear from your sight, to vanish utterly, then you will never be able to face yourself, knowing that Jedidiah trusted you to help him. Please, please, good sir, don't turn your back to me. My troubles crowd upon me and I have none else to rescue me.

MASTER GREEDY: [*He seems deeply affected by Jedidiah's words and turns partly away to hide his pretended emotion. Seemingly mastering his feelings, he finally turns back to the impatient Jedidiah.*] I can control myself no longer. You have touched me deeply.

PASH-HUR: [*To audience*] Did you ever see such a soul of compassion?

MASTER GREEDY: As you should know, this is because I have a natural sympathy for those in great distress, so I'm going to interrupt my busy schedule. From now on all my energies shall be devoted to your case. I say this because there is good hope that Amon's argument that no contract existed between the two of you can be disproven. Hence don't be afraid to take your case to court, for all his arguments are worthless against your claim. Be of good cheer, and in a half-hour's time make your way to my house and there we shall calmly and quietly discuss what I shall argue before the judge. I guarantee that you will not be unhappy with what I'm going to say.

JEDIDIAH: [*Impulsively kissing his hand*] I'm happy just to please you, my dear sir. [*Greedy exits*]

PASH-HUR: [*Stepping forward to audience as Jedidiah looks after the departing lawyer*] Here is this man, drawn only by the lure of a few silver coins. Yet when my master hears only that the man will defend him, he immediately promises him a gold mine! [*Turning to Jedidiah*] At this moment, Master, what are we going to do for money?

JEDIDIAH: I'll use the twenty pieces of silver that I have for buying books as a retainer for his legal services.

PASH-HUR: [*Aside*] Can the lion suddenly refrain from being a beast of prey and lie down with the lamb?

JEDIDIAH: Then I shall pawn this ring of mine and try to find some other way of raising money. There are many ways open to me.

PASH-HUR: Isn't the best way to go directly to the venerable Rabbi Amitai, the head of the Law Academy and your own most capable teacher? He certainly is an excellent counsellor in legal matters. Then you won't have to take a detour where you'll have to pay a heavy toll in coin of the realm.

JEDIDIAH: It's because I respect and revere Rabbi Amitai so much that I cannot bring myself to speak a word to him about my private affairs. Furthermore, I really would have no alternative but to take his advice, even if that advice is diametrically opposed to what my own feelings direct me to do. On the other hand, my attitude towards Master Greedy is vastly different. I can make him do whatever I want, and thrust my point of view upon him as precisely as with this rapier point! But now, before anything else, I must inform my chosen attorney what my father-in-law Amon intends to do, and what is taking place inside his home. Now there can remain no doubt that he has become my enemy. [*He knocks bravely at the door.*]

SCENE IX

JEKARAH, Amon's maidservant, JEDIDIAH and PASH-HUR

JEKARAH: Who's that knocking on my door?

JEDIDIAH: Open the door for us, Jekarah.

JEKARAH: And who are you, sir?

PASH-HUR: Are you so bleary-eyed that you can't recognize my master, Jedidiah, and me, Pash-hur, his servant?

JEKARAH: [*Opening the door a crack, suspiciously*] What are you doing here at this time?

PASH-HUR: Look, you beautiful, foolish woman, doesn't Jedidiah occasionally drop in at the home of his father-in-law?

JEDIDIAH: Come on, open up for me, Jekarah, because I must talk over something with Amon, your master.

JEKARAH: Just a moment and I'll ask. [*The door closes.*]

JEDIDIAH: [*Losing his composure*] Did you notice the way she addressed us, Pash-hur?

PASH-HUR: I took it all in—the whole business. But stand your ground, Master. Remember, we are his enemies, come to burn down his household with torch and kindling. We shall gather an army and attack him with swords, spears and javelins, until, by dawn's early light, he will not even have a wall left to piss against!

JEKARAH: [*The door opens again, the same width as before*] I inquired for him and was told that he has gone around the corner—shopping.

JEDIDIAH: [*Furious*] Whom did you ask? Who answered you?

JEKARAH: [*Shouting back in temper*] With my own eyes I saw he wasn't home!

PASH-HUR: [*Joining in the shouting match*] Look, you wicked, stubborn creature, are you lying to us? Such nonsense will get you nowhere!

JEKARAH: Why doesn't my lord go down the street and ask if I've made up a story?

JEDIDIAH: Couldn't you open the door to me for another reason? I haven't had any word about my sister Shifrah, who's inside living with you.

JEKARAH: I'm sorry, your Honor, but I cannot.

PASH-HUR: And who is it that prevents you from doing so?

JEKARAH: Amon and my mistress who are not at home. [*She slams the door in their faces.*]

JEDIDIAH: [*Unbelievingly*] They are not at home to me and won't welcome my company when I'm practically a member of the family?

PASH-HUR: [*Sarcastically*] Should I not, therefore, take revenge on this Hamen-Amon for the evil that he has done me?

ACT III

SCENE I

BERURIAH and JEKARAH her maidservant

BERURIAH: What shall I do, Jekarah, my faithful friend? My father and mother have taken me from my beloved Jedidiah and have given me to a man whom I don't know at all and whom I can't stand. Has anyone, anywhere, suffered so much misfortune? While still young and innocent, women are thrown at men who are total strangers, while men can pick and choose whomever they like for their wives.

JEKARAH: By the Covenant, it's a terrible affliction imposed by Fate upon womankind. Yet I am also aware of young men, free men, who cannot marry whom they desire. I also have special, secret information that Asael wishes to marry another girl who is as beautiful as the moon. Yet, by his father's order, he must marry you.

BERURIAH: I shall never respect him, for my feelings are elsewhere.

SCENE II

JEDIDIAH, BERURIAH, PASH-HUR and JEKARAH

JEDIDIAH: There's Beruriah, just come to the door!

BERURIAH: [*Continuing to speak, not noticing Jedidiah*] It's Jedidiah that I love, and I hate Asael most intensely!

PASH-HUR: She feels the same way you do.

BERURIAH: It's all my mother's fault. I see that now. It was she who did this terrible thing to me, although she pretends otherwise.

PASH-HUR: Go and have a heart-to-heart talk with her. Then you'll be able to convince her.

BERURIAH: Why don't all Jewish girls complain about this horrible wrong which I am the victim of?

JEDIDIAH: [*Approaching her*] My darling, my beloved Beruriah, today I cannot greet you with a greeting of "peace," because there is no peace in my heart.[17] If I have hurt you, as I fear I have, please my dearest love, tell me what it is so that I can sincerely make it up to you and right the wrong that unwittingly I have committed. Yet if you find me innocent of any wrongdoing, why do you reject my love? Why do I seem so loathesome to you? [*Beruriah begins to weep, and veils herself, as if before a stranger.*]

PASH-HUR: Beruriah, why are you crying?

JEDIDIAH: Why do you veil your face, as if before a stranger?[18]

PASH-HUR: Why don't you answer?

BERURIAH: Oh, mother, woe is me that ever I was born.

PASH-HUR: Her tears are like precious pearls and the fine gold of Ophir, offered on the altar on your behalf.

JEDIDIAH: If some malicious spirit has incited you against me, then let me propitiate him with an offering.[19] For G-d, who searches all our inward parts, knows that I have done no wrong and committed no crime.

BERURIAH: My dear, darling Jedidiah. It is my cruel parents who have been responsible for breaking our engagement that we lovingly made together, thereby leaving me in despair. So let me pray to One who is full of compassion that in His great mercy He will relieve you of your lovesickness and that you will have no more pain because of love for me. As for me, because of my great affliction, because I am split in two like a willow wand for love of you—I pray that G-d grant me the strength to bear the shock of this bitter separation. May He be so merciful as to cause my death, so that I will not have to endure the awful fate that is in store for me.

JEDIDIAH: Is that what you really want to do—to drive me away so that you can become the wife of someone else?

BERURIAH: What can I do in this wretched state I'm in?

JEDIDIAH: Can your father's cruelty reverse your feeling for me and make you hate me?

BERURIAH: G-d forbid that I should hate you, for I am a woman in love, so I am ever concerned for your welfare. I peep from my lattice window to watch you approach, and your very appearance revives my spirit. My praise of your virtues has never been surpassed, for to you I have given what is the very best of myself—a loving heart.

JEDIDIAH: If you mean what you say, then why not spurn Asael? Don't be shy, but do what your heart tells you. For how can I see you snatched from my arms without being consumed by melancholy? If the pain of my suffering does not kill me, then I shall certainly fall upon my sword. And if I commit suicide I shall condemn my soul to perdition as well as my body.

BERURIAH: How can I defy the decision of my parents without completely disgracing myself?

JEDIDIAH: As is customary among the maidens of Israel, you did not demand a particular husband but accepted unquestioningly the one your parents picked out for you, although it is right and proper that maidens be consulted in their choice of husbands. So, you are asking nothing but that they go along with what they orignally told you to do—to accept willingly and lovingly Jedidiah as your husband. Did you not do as they bade you? Now, even if they killed you, you could not turn your heart about and stop loving him.

BERURIAH: Heaven knows that I intended to ask this. But then in order to prevent me, they quickly brought in a messenger without letting me know beforehand. He placed a golden chain about my neck. In my innocence, thinking it was a token of affection from you, I gladly accepted it. Then and there a loud proclamation was made throughout the house that, by accepting the gift I was forthwith betrothed to Asael, the son of Ephron. Upon hearing this announcement, I became petrified with fear. I had no strength left to raise my voice in protest, but remained in a state of shock, my eyes fixed on the floor.

JEDIDIAH: Oh, horrible! I am lost!

PASH-HUR: [Aside] I can just see all the officials there thinking her silence signaled acquiescence to the betrothal.

JEKARAH: No doubt that's what they all believe.

BERURIAH: And before I could recover my senses everyone had gone and I was left alone, alarmed by what had occurred and terrified for what was to happen to me. [Jekarah turns to listen at the door, as if hearing someone inside the house.]

JEKARAH: Beruriah, did you hear anyone call?

BERURIAH: I didn't hear a thing.

JEKARAH: I am sure the mistress is looking for you. I'll go inside and listen.

JEDIDIAH: Are you going to leave me, Beruriah? Stay and speak to me.

BERURIAH: Don't stop me from going or my mother will be furious.

JEDIDIAH: Just wait here until Jekarah returns.

BERURIAH: I can't stay any longer because my mother bade me hurry and be ready to leave for the country within half-hour.

JEDIDIAH: Why? Where are you going?

BERURIAH: I don't know why, but that's what she told me to do. I'm supposed to leave for her sister's vineyard that is a short distance outside the city. I'll be there for a day or two.

JEDIDIAH: One calamity upon another! And my sister who lives with you—is she going too?

BERURIAH: She is not to stir a foot outside her quarters, as well as her two serving maids, but remain under the watchful eye of old Sarah. So I shall be denied her companionship when I depart, and all alone I will have to weep day and night. But at least take comfort that while separated from you I too shall be in exile. While I am gone, remember your faithful Beruriah, just as I, in my heart, shall ever be with you, for my heart is no longer within me, but is beating in your bosom. Don't grieve or feel pain for me, because I suffer whenever you suffer. May an angel watch from Heaven over us and save us.

JEDIDIAH: How can my soul be separated from my body without perishing outright? My love, please don't think ill of me if, by daylight I go in disguise to the country so that once again I may see the bright beauty of your face that quickens my failing spirits.

BERURIAH: Your visit will revive my spirits as well. But I am terrified of my mother's temper, were she to find you there.

JEDIDIAH: I will transform my appearance so that none except yourself can identify me.

BERURIAH: Do as you see fit. But please know that while I openly profess my affection for you, I still cannot violate my honor. Now I must go inside to my mother, for I can stay no longer, much as I should like. Remember me and don't forget an innocent maid. [She goes in.]

JEDIDIAH: Oh, I am like a blind man groping at noon, for whom the sun already has set. Pash-hur, my servant, have you deserted me?

Why is the space about you so dark and sunless? Tell me, what shall I do, where shall I turn, upon whom shall I rely?

PASH-HUR: If you'd put your trust in the lawyer I would choose for you, then you'd soon bring Amon to justice and right the wrong that has been done you.

JEDIDIAH: Were it not for Beruriah, I could easily quench my arrows in the blood of her parents. However, I shall strike a blow against Asael before he steals my sweetheart. I shall draw my sword, kill him, and consign his bloody carcass to the ground!

PASH-HUR: On the one hand, if you deal with him as violently as you say you will, why surely you'll be put to death by the officers of the court and Beruriah will become the wife of someone else. On the other, if you secretly set a trap to catch him, within a day or two he'll learn of your scheme and deliberately take your beloved out of your reach. So, take my advice if you want to get out of this dilemma. It is crystal clear that Beruriah's love for you is stronger than death. Her heart is ever yours. Therefore, since she has not betrayed your trust by unwillingly accepting another man as her husband, why don't you elope with her according to the law of faithful lovers?

JEDIDIAH: But if I did this, would I not be acting most disgracefully, since she is betrothed to another?

PASH-HUR: Your brain has been addled by taps from misfortune's rod! Would you rather kill yourself and so put an end to your soul as well as your body? Do as I tell you, so that you won't have to die! I'll clear the way of any stumbling-blocks. Get hold of yourself so that you will not be blown away by every contrary wind. I'll find a woman from Ever-En-Aday[20] who will cunningly detain Deborah with her long tales, while you carry Beruriah away from her aunt's country place to a hidden refuge of your own. Then will the lily revive and the lovers enjoy connubial bliss.

JEDIDIAH: I can't say whether your plan is bad or good until we go to Master Greedy. I'll report what has happened and hear what he has to say about all of this. Only then will I decide how to proceed.

PASH-HUR: Well, let's get over there with what information we've obtained, and so set your heart at ease. But I'm convinced that he won't give you better advice than mine!

SCENE III

SHOVEL, the newly-rich former slave and OBED, his servant

SHOVEL: Now, Obed, my man, don't be slow in transferring the rest of my goods and boxes into the basement, and get the cloth-of-gold stored on the top floor of the house!

OBED: That I'll do, my lord. For you I have worked magic. No sooner had we landed than I found for you an absolutely splendid residence near the shore and the custom house, with the market handy, as well. Thus, Master, you can transact all your business and transfer goods with no effort.

SHOVEL: Obed, my faithful servant, you know that since I gained my freedom I have enjoyed being an important man of affairs. I love a calm and restful life with an abundance of delicious food and drink. I'm blessed with a most agreeable existence, thanks to the generosity of my former master who died in Damascus. Just before he breathed his last he willed all his posessions to me and made me a wealthy man. So that you may know the rest of my secrets, let me also tell you in confidence that, before the day is out, I shall become engaged to a girl from one of the finest families in the land: she is to become my very own wife!

OBED: Why did you suddenly get the impulse to marry?

SHOVEL: For a man who has risen to a prominent position in the world, as I have, whose sacks are overflowing with gold and silver, it would be a disgrace not to indulge in the good things of this world. As it is written:[21] "Every blessed thing that one can take pleasure in, from it one must not abstain." It happened that while I was going back and forth on business, I spied a girl at the window of a house close to the one I rented for my use. She was radiant as the sun. I found her most attractive and so I shall take her to wife.

OBED: Who is this young woman?

SHOVEL: The daughter of a wise and learned man, a jurist of jurists! His name is Master Greedy, originally from Israel.

OBED: How did you manage to uncover such information in so short a time?

SHOVEL: The fact is that chance brought me in touch with that old woman whom you saw at the door wishing to talk to me. I inquired from her about the girl's background. She reported that the girl came from a distinguished family. I knew how beautiful she was.

So I sent the woman to speak for me to the girl's father. The old woman related that when he heard how wealthy and powerful I was, he did not try to bargain about the dowry, but raised his hands to heaven in assent, declaring that the betrothal should take place as soon as possible. And that's what's going to happen. Now get moving and bring all the goods left in the ship into my house. Meanwhile, I'll betake myself to the home of that leader in his profession and pillar of the community, my future father-in-law, a man of eminence and distinction. There I shall finally get to speak to him, for up to now I have not actually met him. [*He leaves*]

OBED: [*Calling after him*] That I'll do, most admirable and praiseworthy Master! [*To the audience*] Just look at this beast who walks like a man. Observe this ape, this viper, sitting so high and mighty on his royal throne! They praise his glory and majesty as if he were a prince in Israel! Can you imagine? Barely three months ago he was a low-life—a slave, just as I am today. But Satan took a liking to him and raised him up by having Sholom of Sidon, his master, move to a distant land where he took to his bed with a deadly disease. In his last moments he willed all his worldy possessions to this despicable wretch. Now he has the arrogance to display himself in all his finery before the crowd of the town. He really believes everyone in the world is as nothing compared to himself. The earth shakes and quakes beneath the feet of this worthless slave, just because his master left him money. Now another piece of foolishness has entered his head: he has decided to take to wife a daughter from one of the first families of the community. Just as one goes to the market to buy finely sifted flour by its weight, so he is rushing off to get himself betrothed to a maiden according to her family's prominence. Yet, in every way he's a tightwad and a miser. He's like a guest who has pulled on his walking boots and taken staff in hand but still does not take his leave. Who can doubt that his arrogance will grow worse, especially now, in these troubled times, when the whole world worships Mammon and takes money to be the answer to everything. [*Addressing the women in the audience*] Daughters of Israel, would you subject yourselves to so dire a situation just because a jackass wants to live with you? Would you stoop to an alliance with a boor, just to wear gold embroidery? I suppose that now I must do everything he commands, just because I eat his bread. I know remarkably well that this rogue, when angered, can cause more harm to a person than an enraged boar. There's none like him to act the tyrant over his servants, but play the gentleman before his neighbors. [*He exits.*]

SCENE IV

JEKARAH, alone

JEKARAH: I would be justified in calling this place an abomination, a field of slaughter, because from it I have heard no sound but wailing, weeping and shrieking. Whenever I enter my Master's chamber I find him absolutely livid with rage, giving his wife a tongue-lashing, while she, in turn, rails at him. When I proceed further through the rooms I come upon Beruriah lying prostrate upon her couch and weeping bitter tears, with none to comfort her because her precious Jedidiah has been taken from her. When I go upstairs to the top floor, there is Shifrah clutching at me and crying in a still, small voice not to desert her, but get her help. Earlier she had given me a note which I was to convey to Asael, Ephron's son, by means of a trusty messenger, and I promised to do so. But I don't know anyone else to send except my boyfriend, the washerwoman's son. For love of me he would run so fast over hot coals that his bare soles would not even be scorched. [*She exits*]

SCENE V

MASTER GREEDY, JEDIDIAH and PASH-HUR

MASTER GREEDY: If these are the facts of the case under review, then you have three major concerns; the first is whether your elopement would be in violation of G-d's law, and therefore put your soul in jeopardy; the second has to do with the faint-hearted and fearful behavior of Beruriah at the time of her second betrothal; the third is your own fear that, G-d forbid, you would be put to death for having sexual relations with Beruriah. Now, with regard to the first question, I guarantee that your soul will not be forever damned, because the second betrothal ceremony was null and void, since the arrangement was entered into deceitfully and without

Beruriah's consent. My inference derives from the fact that G-d judges a person by what she really feels in her heart, rather than by outward appearance. This is my defense against the eternal damnation of your soul.

PASH-HUR: Could you put down a deposit to guarantee this lawyer's defense will hold up in the Heavenly Court?

JEDIDIAH: This is a great legal principle, in very fact!

MASTER GREEDY: I take it that you intend to save Beruriah from the extreme penalty for adultery? Well, then, the rankest law student knows that when a helpless girl is raped against her will, if her cries of protest cannot be heard at some distance, she cannot be condemned with the man. Thus you may elope with Beruriah and no legal blame can fall on her, since, seemingly, she will have been compelled to go with you by force.

PASH-HUR: [*Aside*] Such an argument, no doubt, can be used to save *her* from disgrace and damnation!

JEDIDIAH: Your advice is very persuasive. But how shall I be able to extricate myself if, Heaven forbid, the public sees us alone together.

MASTER GREEDY: Then pretend to know nothing about the second betrothal. In that way you will accomplish your heart's desire while saving your own skin. To all who question you, say that you have merely ploughed your own field, so you cannot be charged with any crime. Eating a bit of unleavened bread to whet the appetite before the Passover meal is a transgression that demands some expiation. Well, for that amount of sinning you are willing to make amends.

JEDIDIAH: This is good advice, indeed!

PASH-HUR: [*Aside*] He's without compare in that respect!

MASTER GREEDY: She's certified as your wife by deed and oath!

PASH-HUR: [*Aside*] Everyone knows it—she's his bride.

JEDIDIAH: You have found timely solution. Still, there's a large doubt lurking at the back of my mind. Say the matter of our being alone together becomes public knowledge, G-d forbid. Suppose that Beruriah, desperate to save herself, should declare that I made her elope, but also testifies that she had informed me when I took her, that she was betrothed to another. How in the world could my words be believed that I knew nothing of the second engagement?

MASTER GREEDY: I am confident that you can extricate yourself from that situation by declaring it inconceivable that Beruriah, whom all know is your betrothed, should be given to another without your knowledge. Nevertheless, if she would say something to you about being betrothed to another, you could testify that you thought that she was trying to cool your passionate advances by making up so incredible a story.

PASH-HUR: What a smooth, straight course you must run, Master, with no stumbling allowed!

JEDIDIAH: Are you sure, most estimable sir, that you will take it upon yourself to rescue me if I am in distress—that you will come to my aid as you have pledged?

MASTER GREEDY: I shall be your defense counsel, just as I have stated.

JEDIDIAH: I assure you that there will be a substantial fee for your services. What I have already given as an advance in that regard will be only a small fraction of what you shall be getting from me.

SCENE VI

JAIR the apprentice-lad, MASTER GREEDY, JEDIDIAH and PASH-HUR

JAIR: I have been looking for your honor for more than an hour. Only now have I found you.

MASTER GREEDY: Why have you been seeking me?

JAIR: Because there is an official of Israel, wearing garments of high rank, who awaits you at your home. I didn't catch his name, but he is here to see your Honor on very important business.

MASTER GREEDY: I shall be there directly. Jedidiah, my boy. Keep up your courage and I know you will succeed. When you need me I shall be at hand to help you.[22] [*He starts away.*]

JEDIDIAH: [*Calling after him*] I am indeed fortunate sir, to be able to rely upon your services! [*To Pash-hur*] Now, Pash-hur, my man, what are we to do?

PASH-HUR: We must get out of town without delay. So that you may leave safely and surely, let me propose that we exchange our clothes for others. In that way we can disguise our appearance before setting out for the countryside. I'll guide you and point out the way so that you may reach the object of your heart's desire. [*They start to leave.*]

JEDIDIAH: I'll do exactly as you say.

PASH-HUR: Do that and things will turn out all right.

ACT IV

SCENE I

JEKARAH the servant and ASAEL the suitor

JEKARAH: [*Entering from one side of the stage*] I am absolutely worn out from looking about without finding a reliable messenger.

ASAEL: [*Entering from the opposite side of the stage*] From the day I was born I have not encountered anything as confusing as I have today.

JEKARAH: That's Asael's voice. [*She spies him*] It is, really and truly. Welcome, Asael, my lord!

ASAEL: Oh, Jekarah, you are a friend indeed!

JEKARAH: Why are you sighing as if you're worn out with worry?

ASAEL: Because while returning to the city I came upon Jedidiah, Shifrah's brother, hiding in a field with his servant. He was clad in second-hand rags like a highwayman. Suddenly he came down upon me, like a lion on the rampage, with drawn sword in hand, intending to kill me. He killed the horse under me and my legs almost gave out while I was trying to get away. In a fit of rage he was about to murder me, had the Almighty not been with me. I did not wish to kill him, for if I did, as I told myself, how could I hope to win the love of Shifrah, his sister, whom I love. I don't know what set him off against me and made him wish to attack me in cold blood on the highway. Perhaps he was not aware that I have the greatest affection for his sister.

JEKARAH: No, sir. That's not the way things are at all, but the other way round. He thinks you're a rival for the hand of his intended. Here's a long note from his sister, your sweetheart, that reveals the real reason for his anger and gives you the situation in a nutshell. Go back to your room and read the message very carefully, so that

you may learn why he blames you and what led up to his attack.
Now I must leave as I have orders to accompany my mistress to
the country.

ASAEL: I've just met Amon, your Master, riding upon a mule and
followed by a closed cart carrying some women.

JEKARAH: Oh, oh! I'm going to catch it! I must run after them.

ASAEL: And I'm homeward bound to study this long letter. [*They
leave in opposite directions*]

SCENE II

The apprentice-lads JAIR and JOKTAN

JAIR: Soon, Joktan, my good friend, there will be heard in the house
the sound of joy and gladness, the sound of bride and bridegroom,
for our law instructor, Master Greedy, has given his youngest
daughter in marriage to a certain highly esteemed and honorable
man of substance in the community.

JOKTAN: When will we begin to trip the light fantastic and otherwise
have a gay old time?

JAIR: On this very day, old fellow. Let's hope that his son-in-law will
proclaim in the words of the prophet Micah, "And they shall learn
. . . no more,"[23] since Master Greedy will be occupied and won't
be able to keep an eye on us.

JOKTAN: May it be the Lord's will! Amen. What I'm really worried
about is that our Master will impose extra assignments on us to
solve problems and otherwise provide answers to his legal questions. You know as well as I that for the entire month just past we
have done absolutely no study at all and have forgotten whatever
we have learned.

JAIR: With words like these I can keep him happy. For I already
have a question to stump all the experts on Jewish Law when
they try to provide an answer. In the scroll commemorating the
Feast of Esther it is written: "And they hung Haman." Yet in
the chapter dealing with Balak[24] it is definitely written, "And the
children of Israel consumed the manna—that is, in Hebrew, "Ha-
Man, Ha . . . man—Haman" So how could the Jews, who had
been commanded not to eat carrion, eat HaMan, then eat from the
body of the hanged Haman?

JOKTAN: That one I'm up on. The answer that Rabbi Bilaam, the son of Rabbi Bibi, quoting his father, gave was: "What says the Torah?—'And they consumed the mannah,'—that is, Ha-Man . . . Haman." That serves notice on us that in the merry time of Purim, the Feast of Esther, we are expected to eat sweetcakes made of fine flour and oil, and ever after they are to be known by Haman's name. So it may always be said that the taste of mannah was like the honeycake.

JAIR: A fine explanation, originating with Rabbi Bibi of blessed memory.

JOKTAN: You'll see that our good teacher will be satisfied with the way we solve these tricky questions, even if our answer is not strictly kosher. But what I'm really frightened about is that he'll take it into his head to have us compose and learn by heart some long speech praising the bride and groom, so that we may deliver it at the wedding banquet. In that case we'll spend our time just looking at the fancy dishes without being able to eat them.

JAIR: May such a disaster never befall us! Ever! But look! I believe I have a way to get us out of that terrible situation.

JOKTAN: From whence comes our help?

JAIR: I shall let it be known that I have a headache and have taken to my bed.

JOKTAN: I also thought about pulling such a stunt. But on second thought I realized that if I acted like that I still would not be allowed to enjoy myself by sampling the pastries and dainties that are sure to be piled high upon the table. I really would suffer then, if I were deprived of such wonderful foodstuff!

JAIR: There's none smarter than you in anticipting what might happen. Let's think of another remedy for our difficulty, so that we will not have to endure punishment, should this calamity strike us.

JOKTAN: Lo and behold, the Master is leaving the house!

JAIR: I'm getting out of here fast.

JOKTAN: And I'm already out of sight! [*They bolt offstage.*]

SCENE III

SHOVEL the former slave, MASTER GREEDY the lawyer,
and OBED, Shovel's servant

SHOVEL: I am utterly undeserving of the honor that your Excellency bestows on me.

MASTER GREEDY: Rather, my dear sir, the honor of your Excellency is well known to me, for I have lived in the land of Israel and am aware of your splendid reputation. I lived in the Galilee for two whole years.[25]

SHOVEL: I have much to "allude" to your Excellency concerning my natural tendency for generosity.

OBED: [*Aside*] That you will do to increase the illusion of the excellency of your honor!

SHOVEL: Obed, are you attending me?

OBED: At your beck and call, most respected Master!

SHOVEL: Before everything, when you arrive home open the trunk marked No. 13 with the merchandise from southern Israel and take out four bolts of choice mohair. Bring them directly to the house of my esteemed father-in-law. He is a man of most admirable weight in the community. [*Turning back to Greedy*] My lord, you will please me by deigning to accept such trifling stuff and have it made into a fine turban and robe for yourself and your wife, my mother-in-law.

MASTER GREEDY: I beg you not to favor us with these magnificent goods, for we have done nothing to deserve such glorious gifts. Still, we will accept them as a token of appreciation for your famed generosity. That trait of character has made us better persons for having beheld it in you!

SHOVEL: Oh, I am as good as my word! Now, my man, follow my instructions to the letter.

OBED: [*Aside*] When the King's word is law who dares to say, "What's this your're doing?"—to quote King Solomon![26]

SHOVEL: Furthermore, there are two bolts of blue and purple cloth of silk that I put aside. Bring them as my personal gift [*turning again to Master Greedy*]—the first to your dear elder daughter, the second to your darling younger daughter, my finaceé. Kiss her soft and gentle hand for me and tell her how very much I love her and that I am entirely under her spell.

OBED: I shall do exactly as you have bidden me. [*Aside to the audience*] Once you were quick to fret over each piece of silver spent in the purchase of such goods. Now you are not at all concerned about lavishing them on whomsoever.

MASTER GREEDY: [*Aside*] Well, I have found a man after my own heart, of high social position, who will favor me with his generosity for

the rest of my life. He indeed will make my future very happy.
G-d has blessed me through him!

OBED: Just look at him swaggering about, like a king before his troops!

SHOVEL: Most gracious and respected sir, most esteemed father-in-
law: what may I give you to show my appreciation? Ask for
anything and I will get it for you.

MASTER GREEDY: Already I have much, sir, if my wife and daughter
and I have but made a good impression upon you. All my wealth
is yours.

OBED: [*Pointing at Shovel, to audience*] The more he speaks, the more
he increases his gifts.

SHOVEL: Father-in-law, do go back to your mansion and inform your
women-folk that I shall be coming in a little while with precious
necklaces, earrings and rings, so that I may reveal the deep respect
that I have for your daughter when we meet today.

MASTER GREEDY: Do you do so, my dear boy, and I shall summon all
my friends, relations and neighbors together to honor you and to
celebrate this happy event with a party.

SHOVEL: Please don't have anyone of your neighbors over, for modesty forbids me from appearing before so large and distinguished
a company. It is enough if we have only two witnesses of good
character, as is required by law.

OBED: [*Aside*] Well, we'll surely find two witnesses, but of such a
character that they would be ashamed to look each other in the
face!

MASTER GREEDY: Here, again your nicety of taste proves a comple-
ment to your sound judgement. For alone we will be able to enjoy
each other's company, with none to disturb us.

OBED: [*Aside*] What these revelers will gorge upon at this one banquet
could suffice us for a week, with food left over.

MASTER GREEDY: All these arrangements will be assiduously taken
care of. Now I go home to await your coming, my dear sir, and
our celebration.

SHOVEL: If I am delayed, please wait for me. But I'll most certainly
be there on time to the very second. Are you with me, Obed?

OBED: Right at hand. What's there to do? [*They converse silently and
animatedly*]

MASTER GREEDY: [*To himself during this interchange*] Greedy, you
lucky fellow. This very day I have seen wonders occurring.
To think, that at one stroke Heaven has raised me from direst

poverty.[27] This bridegroom of mine is my salvation. In generosity he is a prince and in social standing he is head and shoulders above other men. So he is truly deserving of praise. Because of him, today I have gone from sorrow to joy, and from darkness into great light. [*He exits.*]

SHOVEL: [*Continuing his directives to Obed*] Now, then, get yourself over to the seller of sweetmeats, and with these ten gold pieces buy me the most appetizing and expensive wares. Then place them in a basket and bring them over to the house of my father-in-law.

OBED: It's as good as done!

SHOVEL: Just be careful to choose only the very best that money can buy.

OBED: I'll be absolutely positive to do just that. But would you exchange this coin for me? It doesn't appear to be genuine. [*They remain in silent conversation about the genuineness of the coin.*]

SCENE IV

PASH-HUR, Jedidiah's servant, SHOVEL, the former slave
and OBED, his servant

PASH-HUR: [*Entering without seeing Shovel and Obed. To audience*] Well, today I have really presented the fruit of the tree of life that grows in his private Garden of Eden to my noble master, Jedidiah, for his pleasure.[28] First, I brought him to a grove of golden pomegranates belonging to his betrothed, Beruriah. There he gathered lilies of the valley. And the water stolen from this virgin spring and pure fountain was sweet on his palate, like milk and honey under the tongue. [*Seeing Shovel talking to Obed*] But who is that person? He looks very familiar to me, yet I can't quite recognize him or place where I met him . . . Now I do—that's Shovel, my Master's servant!

SHOVEL: [*To Obed*] Now move and get back fast! You have to be home to take charge of the preparations for all of the festivities and to make sure that everything is properly arranged and ordered.

PASH-HUR: I am shocked at what I see here!

OBED: [*Starting to leave, but stopping to confide in the audience*] I wouldn't exchange all this pomp and ceremony for the glory and adulation owed to an Egyptian courtier, who is exalted by having men run before his chariot, screaming "Make way, make way!"

[*Shovel sees him talking and makes a threatening gesture. Obed disappears.*]

PASH-HUR: [*Continuing*] I'm absolutely flabbergasted! Isn't this Shovel, a slave like myself? Apparently he has dressed himself in expensive garments of the upper crust, just to lord it over me. Just look at the way he measures his steps, like a man of substance, and how grandly he barks out orders to his underlings. And yet he does so in a most foolish, boorish fashion. I'll hail him and see if he responds. Shovel! Hey, Shovel!

SHOVEL: [*Recognizing Pash-hur but then turning away in the hope that he can avoid him*] This is nothing but the voice of a dunce who doesn't understand that I am no longer as I was once, and so doesn't give me the respect now due me.

PASH-HUR: Shovel, give me a friendly word of greeting!

SHOVEL: [*Aware that he can't avoid contact and not sure how to proceed*] Isn't that Pash-hur, the laundryman's son? As far as I am concerned, he's still a common slave. But, come to think of it, it would be more discreet to address him than to ignore him.

PASH-HUR: Hey there, listen to me. [*He still is not quite sure it is really Shovel*] Are you. . . ? Your Excellency will pardon me but I am laboring under the delusion that you may be . . . [*He looks again. Shovel tries to avert his face, but Pash-hur follows him around and finally gets a good look*]. You *are* Shovel and none other. Now really, my dear fellow, what's all this high-and-mighty business? Who dressed you up in embroidered silk? Where did you come from and where are you bound for? Where is Sholom, our Master?

SHOVEL: For your own good I advise you to watch what you say to me, because if you talk too smart, you know what I will do to you!

PASH-HUR: [*Coming close and talking in a confidental tone*] All right. I know that you are jesting with me, as close friends do. . . .

SHOVEL: [*Holding his nose and recoiling*] Why you stinking, miserable villain—I would not have you even wash my feet! Know of a certainty that if you anger me your shoulders shall bear my stripes as a souvenir.

PASH-HUR: Do you expect me to pay you respect just because you are dressed from top to toe in the garments of Sholom, our Master? Come off it, you ignoramus! [*Pash-hur cuffs Shovel*]

SHOVEL: Whom do you think you are, you rotten slave, to dishonor and defame a man like me? [*He gives him a counterstroke of greater force.*]

PASH-HUR: Whom do *you* think you are, you drunkard? A person of your standing deserves a more appropriate position. [*He hits him a blow that wobbles Shovel and drops him to his knees*] And this. [*He hits him another blow that knocks Shovel prostrate.*]

SHOVEL: Woe is me, I am lost. [*He cowers into a tight ball.*]

OBED: [*Running in*] That's my master's voice. [*He sees Pash-hur*] But who's the one beating him?

SHOVEL: [*Advancing on his knees and clasping the ankles of Obed*] Quick, help me!

OBED: [*Screwing up his courage and going close to Pash-hur, in a threatening tone*] Why are you doing this to my Master?

PASH-HUR: This and this [*two rattling blows assault Obed*] will be your lot if you cross me!

OBED: [*Staggering dizzily about*] Oh that I could now glean pleasure as I reap pain!

SHOVEL: Now's not the time for grain-gathering, but for flailing this rogue! You must come to my aid! [*Both men struggle to their feet and together attack Pash-hur. He easily evades their blows and knocks first one and then the other down.*]

PASH-HUR: Two by two you come to me, like impudent dogs to Noah's ark. [*When they move to get up, Pash-hur takes a threatening step and both play dead on the ground. Quite satisfied that they have no flight left in them, Pash-hur departs.*]

SHOVEL: [*Getting up only after he is sure that Pash-hur is well away*] Millions I'll bring against you!

OBED: [*From the ground where he's still lying*] And I'll send zillions!

SHOVEL: [*Shaking Obed*] That's what he's going to get from me, so don't hold me back. [*Obed is trying to free himself from the uncomfortable shaking*] Why were you so slow to help me? [*As Obed struggles to his feet Shovel knocks him down.*]

OBED: I must declare, you're hitting me with a vengeance!

SHOVEL: Where has he gone to?

OBED: Where has your enemy gone to?

SHOVEL: He ran off. I chased him away.

OBED: [*Getting up and dusting himself off*] Have you known him before?

SHOVEL: [*Rubbing the sore spots where he was struck*] We casually came in contact, and now particularly so.

OBED: Who is this fellow who dares to do this to you?

SHOVEL: [*Not listening*] I'll go back to my father-in-law and ask his advice about this serious development, for I respect his opinion.

OBED: Is he, perhaps, the son of your former Master, whose fortune you inherited?

SHOVEL: No, he's not the son, but the slave.

OBED: Are you now going to reveal to your father-in-law that you were born a slave—of a disreputable family—before he gives you his daughter?

SHOVEL: I shall marry her first, and only when she is my wife will I tell him about this unfortunate event that occurred on the way to his house. In that way he'll have to counsel me as to how I should proceed against this man. [*Shovel turns and exits.*]

OBED: [*To audience*] What other way is there? If the best people see that a person has lost his money, no lawyer would take his case. And once a person is down, he's out and unable to again regain his feet.

SCENE V

JEDIDIAH and PASH-HUR

JEDIDIAH: Yes, when I recalled all the pleasures that engulfed my senses while with Beruriah, my betrothed, and the delight in her physical presence when all sorrow and woe was as if they had never been—I confess, at that moment my loins trembled lest I lose my soul and be damned for taking pleasure in excess. For the bliss of the time surpassed even my wildest imaginings. But that's the way of the impulsive human heart: it fulsomely praises improper conduct in order that others may be led in the same way and so fall into error. Yet, the memory of our time together comforts me, for it reminds me that she is mine forever, my destiny, she who can never by shared with another. Why then should I be concerned about any rival for her hand, especially one whose ties to her are tenuous and, what is more, achieved against her will? Then again, Beruriah swore not to belong to anyone but myself when we were betrothed. Yet at the very time I was in a state of absolute bliss, I began to sense that something was amiss. Trembling seized me when I realized that Jekarah, her maid-servant, knew of my presence on the country estate and was trumpeting our secret rendezvous to everyone. This caused me great distress.

Although I had given her present after present, each bigger and better than the last, to keep her quiet, she persisted in wagging her tongue and gossiping without let-up. She's the type who does only what she thinks best! All of this despite the fact that it was I who showed Beruriah how to be happy, and how to avert disaster by taking proper legal steps, on the advice of my attorney. [*Pash-hur has entered.*]

PASH-HUR: [*Aside*] That I'll keep to myself. For the slave who broadcasts such information casts also a snare about the feet of his Master to trip him up and so deprive him of all he has.

JEDIDIAH: [*Emerging from his revery*] Oh, Pash-hur, my trusty man. Because of you I ascended today to the very heights of happiness!

PASH-HUR: May you not descend into a bottomless pit because of an untrustworthy man!

JEDIDIAH: I snap my fingers at the gossip of the town, even though the secret of my rendezvous with Beruriah has been disclosed. No harm is going to happen in spite of everything. You yourself know there is a sure way that we have to restore her honor and virtue, while protecting myself from any harm.

PASH-HUR: [*In a tone of alarm*] That's not quite what's worrying me.

JEDIDIAH: [*Noticing the worried tone*] Why has your face become so sickly green?

PASH-HUR: Because I have seen Shovel your servant, dressed up as a free man with servants flocking about him. He had no knowledge of the whereabouts of your father!

JEDIDIAH: Oh, woe is me!

PASH-HUR: So my Master should hasten to come with me to the judge before Shovel runs away, so that information may be presented that is needed for his apprehension.

JEDIDIAH: When I go before the judge, what shall I say? How shall I ask for justice?

PASH-HUR: Just leave it to me and follow my instructions.

SCENE VI

AMON, JEKARAH, and ASAEL to one side

AMON: What man desires a life of misery, seeing only grief and woe? That's the result of following a woman's advice which is full of snares and traps. Her chambers are dark, and in the public street she makes him look ridiculous and a laughing stock. That's how I am today, completely humiliated and embarrassed. Jekarah, where are you?

JEKARAH: Here I am, hobbling along because my legs are stiff and tired from chasing after you!

AMON: Be sure to inform the judge about everything you observed. Don't worry, because I told you what to say. Just don't make it obvious.

JEKARAH: Everything you told me to say against this wicked outlaw I shall convey. That when he lost his money he also dishonored his good name. But tell me, please. Will my testimony be accepted? For I may not prove an acceptable witness and my testimony may be challenged.

AMON: In extreme circumstances, such as in a capital crime, you will qualify as an acceptable witness.

JEKARAH: May I add something else? That Jedidiah sought to blind my eyes with a substantial bribe and to stop my mouth with a generous gift.

AMON: This, too, you must not hold back, but disclose it as part of your testimony. You must faithfully present everything that you personally heard and saw.

ASAEL: What was that he said?

JEKARAH: Remember this, Master, and don't forget what you promised to give me if I should reveal to the court what it was that Jedidiah said. You said that you would give me double what he said he would give me to keep quiet about the affair.

AMON: What I promised I will fulfill. All I want is to slake my fury by getting back at him!

JEKARAH: If only you saw, as I did, the state your daughter was in— her hair done up in ribbons, a gaily-colored smock about her, her eyes like smouldering coals that are ordinarily the coolest blue. . . .

ASAEL: That's the right way to keep her cool and unassailable.

JEKARAH: Oh, that you had heard her passionate outcries! I know that if you but saw her you would pity her and would kill the one who desecrated her as you would an enemy!

AMON: Before she saw you, did she cry out for help?

JEKARAH: Oh, that unfortunate girl! She had not the strength to raise her voice before I arrived. For Jedidiah, like a sly dog, was stopping her mouth with kisses, and leaving her breathless. Only her lips emited a faint moan, that could hardly be heard.

ASAEL: A taste as sweet as honeycomb!

JEKARAH: But when she saw me you can be assured that she began to attack him with a vengeance, fighting desperately and fiercely to escape his embrace, as from an enemy.

AMON: And as my enemy I'll drive him, I'll push him to the very gates of death. Come on, lets get to the judge! [*He starts briskly offstage.*]

JEKARAH: I'm coming! [*She starts to hobble out after him on her sore feet, then stops*] Oh, Beruriah, I weep for your forlorn state and grievous fate! [*She runs offstage after Amon.*]

ASAEL: My father still rebukes me for not wanting her as my wife. Well, first I'll return to the home of my legal preceptor, the venerable Rabbi Amitai. He is a good man who does good to everyone. I'll present my problem to him. In his great wisdom he will enable me to obtain what I most desire—to wed Shifrah, Jedidiah's sister, who has stolen my heart. But I will not hear a single word against Beruriah, although I despise her father.

SCENE VII

MASTER GREEDY the lawyer, and SHOVEL the former slave

MASTER GREEDY: Now don't worry, my esteemed son-in-law. I have listened to your complaint and understand all the details most thoroughly. I can deliver you from your adversaries; strong though they may be, I shall confound their knavery and, bereft of clothing and possessions, they shall be completely disgraced and you enjoy your triumph over them.[29] All their attacks shall be frustrated; your adversaries will lose hope when they realize that *I* am the one who is championing your cause, so I urge you, "have no fear for I am with you."

SHOVEL: This affair has been a source of much grief to me. But you have made me hopeful of getting out of this mess.

MASTER GREEDY: Here is a list of all the goods that lie in your warehouses under lock and key. Here, as well, is the entire body of testimonials and affadavits attesting to your background and character. So there's no cause to worry that at the trial the judge will find you at fault.

SHOVEL: But that's the very point on which everything depends. For, ever after I shall be known as a former slave—a freed-man. Then

there is also the fact that I cannot hide my identity from my former
Master's son. He now wants to recover for himself the estate that
his father left to me.

MASTER GREEDY: All these contingencies I have foreseen and provided
for. Now collect all these documents and stick them in your wallet.

SCENE VIII

BAILIFFS of the court, SHOVEL and MASTER GREEDY

BAILIFF: There's the man we're looking for! "How the crimes of the
wicked ensnare them!"[30] Grab him! Don't let him get away!

SHOVEL: Woe is me! What's this? What's the reason for all this?

MASTER GREEDY: Why are you tying his hands?

BAILIFF: He'll be coming with us. Those are my orders.

SHOVEL: [*Dropping to his knees and clasping his hands*] Please, please,
dear father-in-law, don't leave me. Good sir, don't run from me,
for you are my last refuge! [*Bailiffs and Shovel leave. Greedy
does not go with them.*]

MASTER GREEDY: [*Calling after the disappearing Shovel*] Go with
them and have no fear, for I shall have you immediately released
from prison. [*To audience*] Really, now, I am amused and unruf-
fled that they believe they can hurt us by such foolish ploys, for
it is a vain effort. [*Even more confidingly as Greedy comes closer
to the edge of the stage*]. But I was amazed when he told me that
he was a liberated slave. Having seen how splendidly and how
richly he dressed, I took him for a man of rank and substance
in Israel. And yet, what sort of a man could get his Master to
will him all his wealth if not one endowed with good sense and
cunning in a higher degree than his fellow? Accordingly, this was
the reason that I speedily arranged his marriage to my youngest
daughter—and for the same reason that I was giving away my
older to Ephron's son—because he was a man of substance. But
I have no regrets in doing so, for I shall bilk him of double the
amount that I originally thought I would get. I shall make certain
that a person of low pedigree will not lord it over my family, but
will become subservient to us. "Shall we receive only good and
not evil?"[31] Consequently, I'll go before the judge and brilliantly
plead the case of my son-in-law, matching argument for argument.

In this way I'll pay back his enemies in kind: they can go to blazes
while we shall prove victorious.

SCENE IX

JEDIDIAH the suitor and PASH-HUR his servant

JEDIDIAH: [*Aside to audience*] My servant Pash-hur and I hastily divided the bailiffs assigned to us by the court into two squads. One
went with me to locate my money and ensure its safekeeping, lest
the slave Shovel spend what he had unsurped from me. I was
confident that the loyal Pash-hur, whom I had left in the courtroom, would disclose any remaining information required to bring
about the apprehension of this villain. But these measures have
given me no comfort.[32] I cannot be at ease, as long as I am so
apprehensive about what my father stated. Indeed my heart fails
me. [*He sinks down upon a bench.*]

PASH-HUR: [*Entering*] Is that you, Master Jedidiah?

JEDIDIAH: [*His head still concealed in his hands*] Of course, it's me!

PASH-HUR: Oh that we were somewhere else, right now!

JEDIDIAH: What terrible news do you bring me?

PASH-HUR: Oh, I am a raven, an evil omen, a veritable wolf that never
bodes good!

JEDIDIAH: Please don't keep me in suspense. Are you predicting
someone's death?

PASH-HUR: Indeed. Death. Your father's.

JEDIDIAH: Woe is me! The very thing I feared has befallen me![33]

PASH-HUR: But there is worse news—even more shocking news. . . !

JEDIDIAH: Who would want to pile even more pain upon me after
such grievous news? Oh, woe is me, father mine, "My head, my
head!"[34] [*He buries his head once more in his hands.*]

PASH-HUR: Woe is right, for on the day he died he made over his estate
to the slave who was at his bedside. Just before he breathed his
last he turned his back upon his own seed and bequeathed all his
wealth to Shovel.

JEDIDIAH: Oh, I am as good as dead!

PASH-HUR: Not only did I have to hear such news through my ears,
I had to see it with my own eyes, as well, personally. When,
finally, they hauled Shovel into court, despite the fact that he cut
a ridiculous figure in the eyes of the officials, he was able to

prove by the original will that he was the rightful owner of your possessions!

JEDIDIAH: What a devasting blow has been dealt me!

PASH-HUR: "They saw and straightway were amazed,"[35] because what he had said proved true. Yet they had no legal way to reverse this unfair decision and to find in your favor.

SCENE X

BAILIFFS of the court, PASH-HUR and JEDIDIAH

BAILIFF: Halt! Don't move, for you are to come with us. The magistrate has ordered that you be made to answer to the charge of rape that has been brought against you by a maiden of Israel: that you did come upon her while she was alone in a field remote from human habitation so that there was none to hear her when she did cry aloud for help.[36]

PASH-HUR: Is not this the final blow that blasts and drives us mad! What more will you do to him, oh cruel Fate, that you have not already done? Will you continue to hound a youth who is guiltless of wrongdoing?

BAILIFF: [*To Jedidiah who meekly accepts the binding of his hands by the bailiffs*] Why do you remain silent like a simpleton? Would it not be better for you voluntarily to confess than be forced to do so?

JEDIDIAH: [*In a fit of any sarcasm*] I am not sorry and feel no regret for what I have done. I have committed adultery. I have even killed two men in the black of night and stolen much gold from the king's treasury. To add to my terrible crimes, I secretly consorted with the enemies of the king to overthrow him. I conspired to murder him and give his carcass as food for the fowl of the air. Now come on, let's go before the judge, because I haven't held back a single thing from you.

PASH-HUR: May I go blind if ever I saw him doing such things!

BAILIFF: Would that I were deaf and did not hear what I heard!

JEDIDIAH: Now there's not a single living soul who can save me. I have chosen death over life. So who's going to tell me what I must do?

PASH-HUR: [*To audience*] I am deeply shocked and pained at this turn of events. [*To Jedidiah*] Oh, Master, most honored Sir: who can relieve your distress or get you out of this fix if you have condemned yourself of your own will. Even should you change your mind, who could save you from execution? Your dearest friends will have nothing to do with you because of your hopeless plight. Amon was the first to turn his back upon you—a not untrustworthy individual. Yet he certainly went back on his word when he took your beloved away from you and changed from a friend to a foe. [*Addressing audience*] Oh you mortals who dwell upon earth, listen and learn an eternal lesson from these circumstances: whosoever is deprived of his wealth and substance loses also the love and friendship of his neighbors, for they no longer have regard for his well being. At this turn of events I am heartsick about my poor Master. He fell to earth like a fallen angel, with none to grant him aid. I should even weep bitter tears for myself—for my own suffering and affliction—because I can't escape the fear that I have fallen into the very trap that I had devised to capture and punish the slave who is now to become my Master. Most assuredly he is going to do the same to me. Night and day he'll take his revenge by oppressing me. Alas whence shall I run for help? Who can advise me how I can save my neck?

ACT V

SCENE I

The venerable RABBI AMITAI, PASH-HUR the servant, and AMON

RABBI AMITAI: In faith I am most grieved that Jedidiah did not first come to me and reveal what had happened: that his father-in-law Amon had declared that their marriage contract was null and void.

PASH-HUR: Doesn't your Honor know that most young men of Israel are hesitant and reluctant to lay bare their secrets before prominent men whom they respect? Yet they are certainly not ashamed to reveal their most private affairs to complete strangers whom they casually meet.[37]

RABBI AMITAI: When it is a matter of utmost import, a man should not be hesitant or fearful. That kind of behavior is stupid and foolish. Even when standing before kings—when it is reasonable to be afraid—a man should still not hold his tongue but disclose what must be said. So now is not the time either for him to be silent or for us to question his behavior. 'Twere best that we rally to his support and save his soul from perdition, provided this is the will of Heaven.

PASH-HUR: From Heaven He gazes down upon earth and espies the suffering of my Master, Jedidiah.

RABBI AMITAI: If this maiden was betrothed by deceit and trickery, as you claim, then we can indeed save her.

PASH-HUR: Here is that very miscreant, Amon, approaching us.

RABBI AMITAI: [*Aside to Pash-hur and the audience*] Let me accost him in a dreadful voice that will pierce his very marrow.[38] In that way I may be able to frighten him into speaking the truth in regard to his daughter's marriage.

PASH-HUR: Wisdom fortifies the wise!

RABBI AMITAI: [*Addressing Amon*] I am very much aware of the crime that you have committed against the son of Sholom of Sidon; thereby you have trespassed against justice, truth and concord. First, you betrothed your daughter to him and later changed your mind. So you humiliated him to such a degree that his youthful anger was naturally inflamed. As a result, in a frenzy of rage—unaware that he was placing his life at risk—he surreptitiously sought to attain his objective by taking an enticing but risky road to the countryside. Do you now heed most carefully what I say and keep it constantly in your mind. You have done violence against your brother when you deceived him. Hence you are covered with shame and reproach, and shall forever be cut off. For this crime you shall have to drink the cup of wrath from the oppressor—the bitter water that swells the belly[39]—and all your household shall be subject to plague, sword and famine! Decent men shall take satisfaction in seeing retribution visited upon your head. Those men who love the Supreme Being who treats the orphan and the oppressed with perfect justice, will rejoice together and celebrate the fact that in His abundant goodness and mercy He will save my client from those who judge him imperfectly on earth. But you will stand apart as one condemned, recognizing your guilt, mourning your children and lamenting your fate.

AMON: Haven't I suffered enough reproach and contempt? Why does your Honor continue to curse me and add to my affliction?

RABBI AMITAI: Because when I realized that your misfortune had come about as a result of your criminal action, G-d said to me, "Rebuke him!"

AMON: You lay your terrible curse on me, a reviled and suffering victim. But what about the man who seduced my daughter when she had already been betrothed to another?

RABBI AMITAI: It will yet be determined whether her betrothal is or is not a valid agreement. Treacherous actions wither and die of themselves.[40]

AMON: Alas and alack! How can I make amends? For nothing is concealed from Him! Most gracious sir, be so kind as to send this servant some distance away from me, for I have something to impart to you in confidence. Would you remove him, please?

RABBI AMITAI: I shall do as you ask. Pash-hur, attend me.

PASH-HUR: Here I am. Right here.

RABBI AMITAI: Please go to a certain scribe and beg him for me to

send along with you a copy of the legal document that Shovel
the slave handed to him when he testified against Jedidiah, your
master.

PASH-HUR: I'll go and return in a twinkling. [*He exits.*]

RABBI AMITAI: And as for you, don't hold anything back from me,
so that I may get all the facts needed for me to do something to
improve your situation. But if you do not tell me all you know,
then I may not be able. . . .

AMON: Really and truly, I wanted to rescue Jedidiah from his terrible
fate, providing I could do so honorably. For I feel very sorry for
him and truly hope that he will not be condemned to death.

RABBI AMITAI: Is that the truth?

AMON: Alas what can I say to convey to you how awful I feel for
holding him up to shame and ridicule—and disgracing my own
good name in the bargain? How humiliated and desperate I feel.
Go ahead—punish me! Don't hesitate!

RABBI AMITAI: Remember well your humiliation, for virtue is not
something that comes and goes. Tell me, what turned around
your good sense and made you do wrong instead of right?

AMON: It was my wagging tongue that I couldn't control. Now were
I to shout in his defense that my accusation was a fabrication and
an outright lie, it still would prove of no avail. For the law states
that an adulterer shall be put to death. There's no defense from
that!

RABBI AMITAI: I realize that it was your anguish that brought ideas of
revenge into your mind, although such thoughts are unseemly in
so virtuous a man like yourself who calls himself a Jew.

AMON: No matter what befalls I shall preserve my honor.

RABBI AMITAI: Well, both honor and glory would be yours if only
you had not let your emotions sway you while investigating an
important matter, but had, instead, let wisdom prevail. For even
in former times when a similar sin of pride overcame many distinguished gentlemen, they did not succumb to grief and despair.
They did not strip themselves of their self-respect, and did not
allow shame to be their attire in the sight of G-d and man!

AMON: Like the shepherd princes of the Bible, the brothers Simon and
Levi who plotted the death of Shechem for having ravished their
sister Dinah,[41] so I, too, shall devise a means of washing the blood
of the condemned Jedidiah from my hands. Then I can remain
untroubled on the great Day of Judgement when the wicked will

be condemned to perdition.

RABBI AMITAI: Why did Dinah's brothers risk damnation in Bible times? In order to rescue their sister from the hands of a brutal non-Jew. But Jedidiah, Sholom's son, is kith and kin—one of our own blood, with whom you signed a binding contract. You will surely obtain your heart's desire if you give him your daughter to wife. You will also save yourself from more of the anger and reproach that he now is directing at you. For love covers all iniquity, should you but give him the chance to be part of your family. Besides, as I have heard, your daughter was actually betrothed to Ephron's son, since it was not done according to proper Jewish law.

AMON: That may be what you have heard, but you were not there to see for yourself! I know for a fact that I can produce reliable witnesses to testify on my behalf. I also can myself testify in court as to what happened. I pray to G-d who gazes down from heaven upon my daughter and sees that she is no longer a maiden, that He may compensate me for the shame done her.

RABBI AMITAI: When the quarrel grows bitter, then should mercy temper anger.[42]

AMON: [*Losing his temper completely*] The earth shall not be appeased except with the spilling of blood! [*He storms out.*]

RABBI AMITAI: From his intemperate remarks I forsee a rough road ahead.[43] When he left he was absolutely livid with rage. However, I have faith in G-d's mercy. In the last analysis, Amon will not deal with us badly, for in his first remarks he seemed to offer us hope when he sought to ease his mind by wishing to do the right thing. Therefore I shall review his earlier statements and perhaps G-d will shed His light upon us and make our path easier to see, so that we do not go astray.

PASH-HUR: [*Returning*] Are you still there, your Honor?

RABBI AMITAI: Where are those documents, pray tell?

PASH-HUR: I couldn't get them copied, for the court clerk refused to let me have the originals.

RABBI AMITAI: Well, then, come along with me, for I have some details to convey to the chief magistrate and the presiding judge. In this critical situation I am confident that hope still exists for us to save Jedidiah's life through the defense that I shall present.

PASH-HUR: [*Breaking down*] If he is doomed to suffer, then don't save his life. For the afflicted life is nothing but grief and pain. If

today he loses his life and is gathered to his fathers, his soul will
enjoy bliss, and he won't see the misfortune that would await him
had his evil father made his life miserable by treating his son as
if he were his enemy.

RABBI AMITAI: Is G-d's hand sparing of salvation? Well, until death
claims me I shall have faith in Him—and even after that. For
even then G-d does not refuse salvation to all who take refuge
with Him.

SCENE II

MASTER GREEDY the lawyer, and OBED, Shovel's servant

OBED: I am very well aware that you handled everything properly and
at the right time, and that your plans worked out successfully and
without problems.[44]

MASTER GREEDY: If it's true, as I've heard, that after he found himself faced with absolute disaster, Jedidiah decided to have himself
executed—well, let's celebrate the successful conclusion of our
plan. For who's going to say him nay?

OBED: It's true that Jedidiah boldly admitted to numerous crimes and
felonies saying that he was weary of life and anticipating death.

MASTER GREEDY: But the problem remains that the closest relation a
person has is himself, and thus his confession cannot be admitted
as legal evidence. Any court of justice would recognize that no
one ordinarily wishes to do himself bodily harm. Such an argument could easily work in Jedidiah's defense, but the way he's
looking to punish himself, it probably won't come to that. I can
just see Satan standing at his right hand, terrifying him with his
baleful presence before toppling him into the abyss to the destruction of his body and soul. Even if the defense should raise the
question: "What man would deliberately do wrong so as to die
with a sullied soul?"—why, every court in the land would convict
a man for such behavior.

OBED: Were Jedidiah to die before his time, like a man who commits
suicide, he could not lay claim even to that small bequest left him
by his father after he willed all the rest of his estate to my master,
Shovel.

MASTER GREEDY: [*Aside to audience*] So, if the poor, miserable Jedidiah dies, my son-in-law stands to inherit even that small portion.

OBED: If only Jedidiah would heed my advice and choose the small bequest for himself, so that at least he might stave off the pangs of poverty.

MASTER GREEDY: What kind of advice is that? Are you suggesting that he claim his father's house?

OBED: If he were to claim the house as his own, then he would only inherit the wind, for my Master would turn down his request.

MASTER GREEDY: Are you urging him, saying: "Go ahead, take your small portion of the inheritance?"[45]

OBED: Even if he were to listen to me, he still would not claim the small portion left him.

MASTER GREEDY: You must know that of all the money left him or its worth in silver and gold metal, he is allowed to accept only one object, according to the terms of the will. Similarly of all the precious stones and pearls of price, he must select only one. And the same goes for the garments of silk and embroidery: he must choose but one.[46] That is to say, of the entire estate he is not permitted to take more than one thing.

OBED: I knew all that! But one piece of his father's estate can remove him from poverty, so that he'll nevermore need to fear its pangs.

MASTER GREEDY: What's this mystery that you're hiding from me? Out with it, there's no one to hear!

OBED: Were he to take my advice, he'd choose as much of the estate as would fit inside a coil of rope. Then at once he'd be at peace.

MASTER GREEDY: Explain your riddle, I'm all ears.

OBED: He'd prefer a hangman's noose around his neck[47]—a measured line[48] that would punish him for his crimes. In other words, to swing upon the gallows!

MASTER GREEDY: Now that is nicely put. As once our ears received the news that Absalom, Solomon's son, was hung upon an oak,[49] so now our eyes will view Sholom's son, Jedidiah, being hung upon an oath.[50] Oh, dear me, how can it have skipped my mind that I was supposed to release a prisoner from jail? Well, I must appear before the judge to obtain the papers for his bail. Then I'll run to the dungeon and free him from his confinement.

SCENE III

EPHRON and AMON

EPHRON: Who is there that does not recognize that your reputation has
not been dishonored, since no man can impart honor to his name
except through the excellence of his reputation? Well then—the
slander of a wicked person cannot harm a blameless person. Even
were your honorable daughter to have had aspersions cast upon
her reputation, how by this have you done wrong or been guilty of
a criminal act? You yourself know the proud spirit of the young
people of our time and how arrogant they are. My son is just like
all of them. When he heard the slanderous gossip concerning your
daughter whispered about, he broke off with her and decided not
to go ahead with the marriage, although such a liaison would make
him very wealthy. Despite the munificent praise that I personally
lavished upon you to the effect that your early reputation had not
undergone a decline, his ears were as closed to my words as is a
viper's. So, defer to me as to a brother, put your trust in G-d, for
it is He alone who can calm the distressed mind of Beruriah, your
daughter, and grant her happiness.

AMON: Woe is me for my misfortune! How did a pure and modest
maiden become a harlot? Please, my dear friend, afford me honor
in public and don't shame me in private by revealing my secret to
your son Asael, who has so embittered my life, even if he really
did not mean to do so. Deal kindly with me and allow me the
favor of your friendship and brotherly love, so that the leaders
of our community may trust me. For you personally have not
rejected my daughter by breaking the betrothal contract that you
concluded with me.

EPHRON: Well, it shall be as you say. I shall keep my lips sealed.
No one shall know about it or learn of its existence. For when
everyone minds his own business, then there is peace.

AMON: So then, come with me before the judge and testify for me
as a member of my family whose reputation has been besmirched
by this man. When I make a complaint against him and plead for
justice on the witness stand, you can confirm what I have said. For
we have made a compact, you and I, that my daughter Beruriah,
whose good name has been sullied by this man, was engaged to
your son, Asael.

EPHRON: How can I testify that a man is guilty of deceit when he is innocent of any wrongdoing? Moreover, you know yourself that the judge will believe the other witnesses who will testify that your daughter formerly was betrothed to another man. Rape is a capital offense, and G-d save me from perjuring myself in such a case.

AMON: Did you not say that we should stick together and go ahead with the arrangements for uniting our two families? That it would be best to confirm the betrothal with a marriage?

EPHRON: It is true that I accepted your daughter as a wife for my son, and that I urged him to comply with my wishes in that regard. Still, that is not the major cause for his changing his mind and refusing to marry her. Now I thank G-d with all my heart that he did not marry her and so have to separate by obtaining a bill of divorcement.

AMON: Who would believe that I should hear such words of reproach from you?

EPHRON: And who would tell me to perjure myself and bear false witness? Wouldn't any person living respond with a feeling of anger to such a request, as I do now? To tell you the truth, when I realized that I had closed my eyes, that I had failed to inquire into the details of the situation at the time of our agreement, I privately resolved not to become upset at your folly. Therefore, as I did once, so now I wish you well.

AMON: Alas and alack, I am undone! G-d has found out the awful things I have done today by taking my wife's advice! She is a veritable Lilith, a Satan on my right hand. But when she comes back from the country, oh will I punish her for all her misdeeds! [*He exits.*]

EPHRON: [*To audience*] I am sorry for all his distress and misery. But who can help him at this point? It is not right for me to perjure myself, just to do him a favor.

SCENE IV

BAILIFFS of the court, EPHRON

BAILIFF: So, I have finally located you in the public streets. Where's your eldest son?

EPHRON: Why are you seeking him?

BAILIFF: Because that's what the judge ordered me to do—to look for and find the two of you and to bring you both before him.

EPHRON: Do you have any information as to why the judge wants to see us today?

BAILIFF: I have been led to believe that it is for a matter not directly involving you that you are summoned to appear, but to furnish testimony about a lad who is on trial for his life.

EPHRON: Return to the courthouse and I'll be there in a little while.

BAILIFF: I can't leave you; you have to come with me. Those are my orders.

EPHRON: I obey your authority. Let's proceed before the judge.

SCENE V

JEKARAH, Amon's maidservant, alone

JEKARAH: Because of the distress of my mistress I have run away. When she returned from the country with her daughter, whose reputation has been lost, my master met her at the threshold to the house. He was like a raging bear that has lost its cub, a terribly maddened, raging animal, for he began to inflict injury and pain with his biting sarcasm. He even went so far as to say, "Aren't you the one responsible for all our shame? Didn't you cause all the awful things that ruined my daughter's name and destroyed me?" It was when he raised his hand to beat her within an inch of her life that I left home. I did so because I dreaded his rage and didn't want him to harm me as well. Also, I couldn't stand to see my mistress' misery and pain, and Beruriah's bitterness, whose reputation has been besmirched. She remained in her room, uncontrollably weeping and crying salt tears. Only her lips were moving—perhaps to curse Jedidiah in a voice weak with suffering. I will not return home until his fury subsides. When they ask whither have I gone—only then will I return. Meanwhile, I propose to start out by going to the launderer's to see whether the dirty clothing has been cleaned. Thereafter I'll drop in at the weaver's, which is much frequented by friends of mine, where I can listen to their conversation and share in the gossip.

SCENE VI

PASH-HUR and OBED, the servants

PASH-HUR: I would not at all be surprised if Master Greedy the lawyer took the side opposite to that of my Master, Jedidiah. He had, after all, concluded a marriage contract that gave his daughter to Shovel; hence it would have been to his great advantage to do so. But I would consider it absolutely shameless and reprehensible had he twisted his own words about in a twinkling, thus diverting advice given to Jedidiah for his defense to serve his own purposes, as if my Master had never been his client.

OBED: That's the way of every blessed lawyer. Confidential information he uses for his own benefit, and so gains supremacy over his neighbors. Yet all the while that he is speaking lies he seems to be concerned only with your welfare.

PASH-HUR: Did you hear all the anger directed against the worthy Rabbi Amitai after he began to investigate the case and give it his special attention? By his wisdom he was able to correct a situation that Master Greedy had perverted by his foolish counsel.

OBED: I am not terribly smart about legal affairs, but it seems to me that many litigants go to Master Greedy for advice on legal procedures. They are tireless in chasing after him and they are far greater in number than those who make use of Rabbi Amitai's legal services. This is because Rabbit Amitai settles his few cases calmly and quietly.[51] But this Greedy is a man who knows how to employ rhetoric and twist words to his advantage. He gives the appearance of being learned in the seventy aspects of the law. He immediately gives the impression that he is an expert lawyer to his very finger tips, and a practiced public pleader.

PASH-HUR: What advantage has an orator with all his eloquence if he cannot prevent a miscarriage of justice? The mightiest speaker cannot save anyone by sheer lung power and windy phrases. But wisdom imparts strength to the wise, while it is missing from the shouts of the crowd when it is aroused and angry. Who is more wise in settling disputes knowledgeably and truthfully according to law and tradition than Rabbi Amitai? Who is so consummate a master of its three sources—the Bible, the Mishnah, and the Talmud? Even when many contest his interpretation or take an oppostie position, he does not retreat from their attack, but proceeds against them on the basis of established precedent and principle. So he wins a case by his intellect, insight and respect for the truth. But what I have observed with my own senses is that Greedy does not speak out of knowledge, but rather toys with words of imprecise meaning, turning them around until their original sense is lost. Hence in his hands the wicked do not get their just deserts.

OBED: Although I am but an ignorant man, unlearned in scholarship, I can vouch for the fact that Rabbi Amitai is a man of integrity. He is greater, indeed, than other learned men in his wisdom and understanding, and in his dedication to justice and truth. Even if many take an opposite position[52] to his and belittle the true words that he speaks, Rabbi Amitai wins his case because of his brilliant mind. Whatever he does, moreoever, he does with a good reason. He does not open his mouth to speak idle words. Consequently the clients whom he has successfully defended sing his praises.

PASH-HUR: I have confidence, then, in his ability to have a prisoner released from prison. But what about us? Our complaints have had no effect, so far. Our condition is ignored. What happens to us is not considered.

OBED: We are in the same boat. One is compelled to slave for Shovel, who, if he gets out of jail, will continue to show the servant who is Master. The other is forced to slave for Jedidiah, provided he escapes death.

PASH-HUR: From neither of these burdens of servitude is there hope of escape. Therefore, it is right that while we are in the same condition we conclude a mutual pact. Each is to help the other so long as he shall live and until death do him part!

OBED: Long live our compact! It shall exist without a shadow of a doubt!

PASH-HUR: Please answer this question. How may I escape Shovel's wrath, if the court reverses its decision and finds in his favor? For then I become his slave!

OBED: Surely G-d would not make Shovel prosper just so he could gain mastery over you. For he will not hesitate to punish you severely for the time when you hit him with your fist.

PASH-HUR: I can't be saved, now that Jedidiah's fortune has vanished, and with it his power to be of influence in the world. That's the reason I went with him to the country—to be his go between and to help him. I want to serve him all my life.

OBED: You'll wear yourself out trying to get out of a hopeless situation.[53]

It's one where you can't sort things out or even tell good from bad. It's one where you are blinded and deafened, where your eyes are dazzled by wealth and possessions in abundance, and where pride mounts like the furnance-smoke of Sinai!

PASH-HUR: Oh, You who dwell in the heavens, why is Your help so slow in coming to crown once more that noble youth, Jedidiah with the wealth and position that is his due. Now this starving body casts about for bread that is nowhere to be found!

OBED: Perhaps G-d will shine upon you and make me happy also. Up to now He has made me shoulder a load that I can hardly bear.

PASH-HUR: Let's go back to the magistrate to see how things have developed in the courtroom.

OBED: I'll come along with you to see how it will all end.

PASH-HUR: May it all end in a feast! [*Rubbing his stomach*]

SCENE VII

AMON, alone, to the audience

AMON: Look! Look! Go ahead, look! You see a man who once was so bold as to marry a stubborn woman. She gave me the fruit of her evil counsel,[54] and her evil eye forced me to take her advice. So I gave in and handed over the fruit of the tree to her and she did eat of its wickedness. Then was my heart deeply troubled within me, because I was slow to recognize how a woman can hem in a man with so much trouble. She's truly, as the old adage has it, "the devil's chariot and the root of all imperfection." But here's Ephron coming towards me. Since he previously snubbed me, why shouldn't I get back at him now?

SCENE VIII

EPHRON and AMON

EPHRON: I know that G-d who answers the afflicted will restore joy to your heart.

AMON: The only joy for me now is that you come as the harbinger of my death, for whom I call and than whom no redeemer is closer.

EPHRON: Only listen to my glad tidings and you will rejoice. For He who made the hills green with verdure will prosper and save you.

AMON: How then shall I be saved?

EPHRON: First I shall propose a question and let me know your answer. Suppose the court should desire to have compassion on Sholom's son and make him even richer than he was before. Would you surely give your daughter to him in marriage?

AMON: Why are you asking about something miraculous—an utter impossibility?

EPHRON: If indeed he could be saved and should recover his wealth— would you still refuse to give your daughter to him in marriage?

AMON: I would not withhold my daughter from him, were I to see but the remotest fraction[55] of that fortune.

EPHRON: Show me your hand and lets shake on that. [*They do so with the palms clapping*] You will be a truly happy man, for while your daughter was pining away a short time ago in despair of ever being joyful again, now she has recovered her reputation. Very soon she will be able to dance blissfully at her own wedding, dressed in the gown of a bride.

AMON: Whose saving voice do I hear behind all of this?

EPHRON: G-d allots merit through a man of merit. The venerable Rabbi Amitai delivered Jedidiah through his wisdom.

AMON: Please don't hold anything back from me!

EPHRON: Well then, listen and you shall know for yourself. To begin with, I am happy for you on two counts. The first is that the shameful action of the sly Master Greedy was publicly revealed. He fell into the same trap that he set for me. Now he runs about after me, but is repelled by my contempt. The second is that one who is raised above all blessings and praise—our exalted and venerable Rabbit Amitai—found a way to alleviate the misfortune that befell you. He did so by pitting his superior intelligence against the perverse Master Greedy. At the outset you must realize that your close friend, the late Sholom of Sidon, did well when he left his wealth to his servant Shovel. All the Master's goods were placed in the servant's hands while Sholom was abroad, so that they would not be squandered. Furthermore, that venerable sage without peer, Rabbi Amitai, showed the sharpness of his legal mind to the people of this land and its leaders. He proved that Sholom deliberately allowed his servant to own all he had—down to the last thread and shoe-lace—with a small exception.

AMON: What I find difficult to understand[56] is why he clearly gave everything to Shovel, his servant of long standing, yet allowed

Jedidiah to claim only a single, small parcel of his estate?

EPHRON: But good things come in small parcels! For, upon the advice of the venerable Rabbi Amitai, Jedidiah chose as his small share of the inheritance the slave Shovel who had been owned by Sholom, Jedidiah's father! Now, whatever a slave acquires, by virtue of the deed of gift, belongs to the Master—that is, to Jedidiah, the heir apparent. So Jedidiah should be a happy man because of the fortune that is not at his disposal.

AMON: I'm amazed! I can't even open my mouth I'm so astonished!

EPHRON: Don't be suprised at the way his fortune was inherited. That idea came from the legal genius of our time, Rabbi Amitai. His actions are always done in the name of Heaven; his ways are enlightened for G-d is with him.

AMON: Good begets only good.

EPHRON: So under court subpoena he brought me to testify concerning Asael's marriage—the one to which my son did not give his consent. Then the magistrate decreed that your daughter be given in marriage to Jedidiah. Since he is of age and a responsible man, he cannot divorce her. All of this the court said should take place, providing it is agreeable to you.

AMON: Is what you say really and truly so?

EPHRON: Wait a bit and you will recognize that I am telling the truth. By the time that I had left the courtyard of the king's palace, a bailiff had already been sent to fetch up the slave from the dungeons so that Sholom's son could formally pick what part of his father's estate he wanted, in the presence of the court. Vast throngs of people were assembled from all the quarters of the city, pressing against each other, the better to see the young man and to join in celebrating his good fortune.

AMON: I am most grateful to you for you have given me comfort. But would you do me two great favors?

EPHRON: Ask. What can I do for you?

AMON: First, make peace between young Jedidiah and myself, for I have recently done him wrong. Second, reconcile Deborah, my wife, with me, for I struck her in a fit of anger.

EPHRON: Indeed you did wrong to your wife, for among us Jews it is a shameful act to strike a woman. For women are tender creatures who cry easily. Nevertheless, I shall come to your house to relate to your wife everything that has happened, and I shall have a heart-to-heart talk with her, and so reconcile the two of you.

AMON: Would it not be best to go first to the court and to right the terrible wrong that I have done Jedidiah?

EPHRON: Why not try to do what the venerable Rabbi Amitai already has done, He who loves and pursues peace? He drew anger from Jedidiah's heart and cast the wrong that you did him into the depths of the sea. Well, I shall accompany you there, but afterwards I shall leave so as to accomplish the reconciliation with your wife, as you bade me.

AMON: Yes, let it be as you have said.

SCENE IX

JEKARAH, alone

JEKARAH: I have chosen a long way to escape from a house of mourning in order to find a happier home. But it is a way that weaves back and forth like a weaver's shuttle, going farther and farther away from the one I have loved. Really, I am not all that distressed by the misfortune that overtook my master's daughter. After all, nobody's going to shed a single tear were I to be overrun by a horde of porters or a host of warriors. I wish now that all my life I had the wisdom just to eat, drink and be merry, for that is our portion in this world. From what I have observed, whosoever chases after happiness, sadness flies from him. Look here. Just yesterday I came upon a most favorable sign. While resting by the road, I found myself wanting to feel a sense of goodness and happiness once again. I was joyful—misery and gloom gradually disappeared upon my hearing a tumultuous shout from the city— a sound coming from the court of justice: Jedidiah had won his case. He had achieved joy and happiness: the wrong done him had been made right. So, I feel that this is most propitious, for on a lucky day like this I, too, shall have luck! Well, I'll go back home and beg Shifrah to make peace between her brother Jedidiah and myself, in spite of the fact that I testified against him at the trial.

SCENE X

The venerable RABBI AMITAI, JEDIDIAH the suitor, and AMON

RABBI AMITAI: Although both of you plotted to place an obstacle in the way of a righteous man, God reckoned it for good. His mercy and truth have not deserted you and He has translated impudence into modesty of spirit.[57] Therefore He will not requite you for your devious behavior in any degree, for Beruriah's love has rendered it honest. Now, as well, her compassion will combine with that love to form golden links in a chain that will join the two families and make them one.

AMON: I would that Jedidiah were as completely sympathetic to me as I am to him. He appears to be set against me and his glance in my direction is hostile.[58]

JEDIDIAH: G-d knows that it was not I that caused our estrangement, surely.[59] Who was it made me lose my head and become reckless? Was it the Almighty who embittered and rankled me, so that I acted improperly?

EPHRON: He's moaning for his dead father, so don't make any response to his questions.

AMON: [*Only too anxious not to cause Jedidiah further upset*] Wouldn't it be best for us to enter my house so that Jedidiah may rest and recover from his terrible ordeal? There all of us can hasten to comfort the mourner with our company and with kind words.

RABBI AMITAI: Let us do as you say. [*He sees Obed, Pash-hur and Shovel emerging from Amon's house*] As soon as these three servants have left the house, we shall say more on the subject.

EPHRON: But first I shall present myself to your wife, as you requested me to do.

AMON: Yes, please do this before we get there. [*Ephron leaves the group and enters the house*].

SCENE XI

OBED, SHOVEL and PASH-HUR, the servants, the venerable RABBI AMITAI, AMON and JEDIDIAH; later, MASTER GREEDY

[*The rich garments have been removed from Shovel and replaced with those more proper to servants. Pash-hur, however, is now wearing the rich garments of Shovel. They stop before Amon's door.*]

OBED: How can it be, Master Shovel, that your lofty social position has been lowered, and that you are now just like the rest of us who are Jedidiah's servants?

SHOVEL: Kill me, for death is better than life!

JEDIDIAH: [*Observing the servant's conversation with the others, some distance away*] Slaves now lord it over him, and he has become their laughing-stock![60]

PASH-HUR: Was ever heard so great a thing—that your highness has fallen so low? Why did you remove that splendid coat of many colors that now I wear?

RABBI AMITAI: [*Interrupting the servants*] Come, now. Let's console Shovel, as well as all others who mourn. May he have peace of mind, for his father-in-law, Master Greedy, was terribly disappointed in him for his loss of status.[61] When last I saw him he looked utterly dejected because of the misfortune that befell his son-in-law, whom he had once greatly admired. He is in a state of shock that Heaven had disclosed his perverseness when he made a betrothal contract that did not specify which of his two daughters was to be married. Now, as a result, both of his daughters require separate bills of divorcement from Ephron's son.

PASH-HUR: [*Seeing Master Greedy approaching*] And you, you slimy shyster, you come just at the right time. Please deign to recognize the lofty eminence of your son-in-law, that noble gentleman, Shovel, Prince of the Underworld!

MASTER GREEDY: Look around you gentlemen, and see if there is anyone who suffers more than I. Now these disreputable slaves are ridiculing me—people whose ancestry is so despicable that I would not even keep them with my sheepdogs.

PASH-HUR: May such a state await you!

RABBI AMITAI: Well, don't fault us for your ills but your evil passion to amass wealth. How can anyone who has placed his soul in peril of damnation be angry, except at himself? Lo and behold, your rash judgements and evil actions have brought you nothing in return. Your wicked quest to have your elder daughter marry a man who did not want her, and your younger daughter to marry a wretch whose family was unknown has brought you to this state of derision. You have no one to blame but yourself. Let all ignoramuses who lust after Mammon look on your folly and take heed. They will realize that it is far better to ally one's daughter with a praiseworthy individual of solid background than to tie oneself to a gold and silver-laden jackass,[62] devoid of spiritual quality and substance.

MASTER GREEDY: [*Beating his breast*] Verily I have done wrong. What can I say? These things I shall be sorry for and lament the rest

of my born days. My daughters are suffering greatly for what is
my transgression. If only their punishment would afflict me alone.
Then would I keep quiet and complain no more.

RABBI AMITAI: It is established in our tradition that a child shall not
bear the punishment for a father. Therefore, I shall endeavor
to find a means of releasing your daughter from her unwelcome
marriage to Ephron's son. I shall exhort him to annul the betrothal
agreement, and I know that he will not refuse my plea. Also, I
know that Jedidiah, because he is the merciful son of a merciful
father, will respond affirmatively to my request that he free Shovel
and provide him and his wife, your daughter, with enough money
that they may be spared a life of poverty.

JEDIDIAH: [*Emerging from Amon's house*] A thousand silver coins I
shall give your daughter as consolation. And you, Pash-hur, sever
your shackles and go free. For such is the judgment of the generous; do good even to the undeserving. For that reason you,
especially, my faithful Pash-hur, deserve to be set free to do good
for others. You shall be a guest at my table all the days of your
life!

PASH-HUR: [*Deeply touched and sinking to his knees in gratitude*] May
I continue to enjoy the favor of my Master.

SHOVEL: [*Also sinking clumsily to his knees in imitation*] How can I
begin to thank my Master?

RABBI AMITAI: Be aware, Jedidiah of what I have known for some
time. My student and your friend, Asael, Ephron's son, now has
told me that he has always wanted to do—to take as his wife
your sister, Shifrah. He will be able to divorce the daughter of
Master Greedy, that despicable lawyer, for Ephron only employed
the marriage in order to recover the deposit of money that was
entrusted to the lawyer to hold for distribution to the poor of the
community, which he did not do. Now, if you will heed my
advice, and if his father will agree—as I am sure he will—don't
stop her from marrying him.

JEDIDIAH: There is good reason for me to fulfill his heart's desire.
That is, providing, of course, that my sister still wants him. For I
see a good man in him and beg his pardon because I once thought
ill of him and sought to do him harm.

RABBI AMITAI: "As it is said," in Isaiah's words, "this is a good
union!"[63] So let us proceed from one good deed to another!

JEDIDIAH: Are you there, Obed?

OBED: Right here, Master!

JEDIDIAH: All these fine clothes of mine are my gift to you. For I shall wrap myself in black until the seven days of mourning for my father are past. But you shall remain close by my side, like a brother, until I can acquire another servant. Then you, too, shall go free.

OBED: May my Master increase in strength and live forever!

RABBI AMITAI: And you, Master Greedy, your honor has been restored. Go home, you and your son-in-law, Shovel, who has been freed from slavery. G-d has removed your shame and healed your wounds. But we shall enter Amon's house to rejoice and be glad together.

[*There is a brief dance anticipating the impending nuptials, at the conclusion of which Greedy and Shovel depart for their home, and Amon, Jedidiah and the rest go through the doors into Amon's house. Following the dimming of the lights and the seven pulses of a drum, the lights come up. The seven days of mourning are over, and a double wedding is held under two traditional marriage canopies, one for Jedidiah and Beruriah, the other for Asael and Shifrah, with Rabbi Amitai presiding, all in pantomime-dance form.*]

NOTES

1 Characteristic of the delicacy of Italian Renaissance Hebrew is the sub-
   stitution of the term "suitor" for a term equivalent to the more blatantly
   sexual *amoroso* of the Italian *commedia.*
2 Here *Hokhmah* is an allegorical personification. As used by Leone the
   term is the equivalent of the Neoplatonic *Sophia* of the Greek and *Sapi-
   entia* of the Latin. Such figures were frequently corporealized in Italian
   Renaissance pageantry. Her raiment is similar to that described for Wisdom by Cesare Ripa in his *Iconologia* of 1593.
3 The traditional Jewish blessing upon hearing unusually bad news.
4 The Hebrew wording has been deliberately selected to remind a learned
   audience of the state of Job.
5 Leone has created a droll word play upon "a voice is heard in Ramah,
   Rachel crying for her children." The Hebrew word *ramah,* when used
   as an adjective to modify the noun, "voice," means "loud." Ramah, of
   course, is the name of a high place (as is implicit in the word itself, which
   signifies "high") on the road to Bethlehem.
6 The Yeshivah or traditional school for training scholars in Jewish law.
   All Jewish young men were grounded in the study of the Bible, Talmud
   and post-Talmudic rabbinic commentary and responsa. That study began,
   ordinarily, about the age of five with exposure to the Five Books of
   Moses. As used here by Leone, the Yeshivah constituted an institution of
   higher Jewish learning, taught by the community's leading Rabbis, who
   served as lawyers and judges for its legal matters.
7 Jedidiah's training has evidently included some exposure to Jewish mysti-
   cism, for his allusion to Beruriah, her beauty and her actions, demonstrates
   a familiarity with the Neoplatonism then current in Jewish scholarly cir-
   cles.
8 A parody of Hebrew love poetry, itself derived from Arabic models and
   from the Song of Songs of Jewish provenance.
9 A curse stemming from Levantine folklore, in which an imp or malevolent
   spirit could be sealed off within some solid object and so prevented from
   doing mischief.
10 Meaning after dark—here a mannered style of expression, of a piece with
   Master Greedy's full-blown, cloudy rhetoric.
11 A child by other parents, found by Sholom and brought up in Sholom's
   household, though not formally adopted by him.
12 The biblical allusion to the fowler's snare can be found in Psalm 124:7.
   The fox is a familiar symbol for destruction, as in Lamentations 5:18.
   Since fowling by net (or snare) for small birds was a practice of hunters
   that was familiar to Leone, he has here incorporated Renaissance aphorism
   with biblical metaphor to enhance poetic effect.
13 The science of physiognomy, based upon Galenic humors psychology,

was initiated during the Renaissance as a means of detecting a person's true character from the permanent set of his or her features. Based upon the facial expression for greed, the actor portraying Master Greedy would be careful to reveal this spiritual characteristic upon his own features. For further explication of this theory as it was applied in rhetoric and the fine and performing arts, see my *Classicistic Acting* (Lanham, Maryland: University Press of America, 1984), pp. 71–83, 97–98, and 102–112.

14 The Gentile custom of a male admirer sending idealizing love poetry to a lady as a token of his regard was also practiced by those Italian Jews who, like Leone, had received a humanistic education. Leone himself wrote his bilingual *Defense of Women* in this same Platonic vein.

15 The youngsters are beginning their studies as apprentices to Master Greedy. Here Leone seems to be paralleling the system of professional training that prevailed in the Gentile community. Since in the Jewish world the rabbi (the scholar of Jewish law) assumed the function of judge, but not ordinarily that of advocate, such an apprenticeship system was hardly regular practice. It is probable that Leone did so for other reasons. One such might have been to imitate the characters already present in Italian comedy, particularly the superficially learned pedant who was regularly provided with apprentices for greater comic effect. Leone also might have utilized the lawyer's guild system of the Gentile world to create an ideal community that would normalize the usually strained relations between Jew and Gentile, and so permit social and legal harmony to exist between the two groups.

16 Leone has placed his play in the ancient world when, as in the time of the Bible, Jewish law sanctioned a limited polygamy. He also has his characters assert a contemporary rabbinic rationale as to why polygamy— even of a limited sort—was inadvisable: because it tended to destroy that domestic concord which was the ideal basis for Jewish home and family life.

17 The regular Hebrew greeting is with the word, *Shalom*—"peace." Hence Leone is playing with words. ("I cannot greet you with *Shalom*, because there is no *shalom* in my heart.")

18 Biblical practice still current among Levantine groups.

19 An inappropriate action for a religious Jew. The transports of love, apparently, have carried Jedidiah away for the moment into the domain of folk-superstition.

20 An attempt to counterpart, for the English reader, the form and substance of the nonsensical place-name, "Ad-Olamit." A similar sounding place name is found in Micah 1:15, and it is likely that this reference provided the basis for Leone's Hebrew pun.

21 In the Purim carnival spirit, Leone makes Shovel see greed and gluttony as sterling virtues, sanctioned by his misquotation of rabbinical ethical

literature.

22 The Hebrew original is a borrowing from II Samuel 18:3. A know-ledgeable audience would recognize the source and thereby the fact that Master Greedy was comparing himself with King David who, by his people's request, remained behind the walls of his city in safety until danger threatened them, when he would emerge at their call.

23 In the Purim carnival spirit Jair has deliberately omitted the word "war" from the well-known quotation of the Prophet (Micah 4:3) to sanction his schoolboy dream of a perennial holiday from lessons.

24 It is nowhere so written. Leone, in the Purim carnival-jester's spirit, makes things topsy-turvey. Numbers 22 nowhere treats of mannah, which sustained the people of Israel in the wilderness. The chapter, however, does describe the activities of the soothsayer, Balaam, whose services Balak, king of Moab, enlists to curse Israel. Just as the untaught Jair cites the wrong source, so the equally untutored Joktan confuses Balaam of the Fourth Book of Holy Scripture with Rabbi Balaam, son of Rabbi Bibi of the Talmud. (Tractate Purim). All of these drolleries were to the delight of an audience alert to Jewish literary subtlety.

25 The Galilee was the seat of Jewish erudition in Talmudic times. The brevity of Master Greedy's stay there is another indication of the super-ficiality of his legal training.

26 There is no such quotation. Again, here is another example of Purim nonsense.

27 An odd, hence witty, conjunction of well-known phrases from the Psalms on the analogy of the Hallel ("thanksgiving") prayer regularly recited in the synagogue on the joyous holidays.

28 At once a parody of Genesis 3:9–12 and of the Song of Songs, particularly 4:12, and of Hebrew love poetry in general.

29 A paraphrase of Isaiah 41:11.

30 Proverbs 5:22.

31 An abbreviated form of the quotation from Job 2:10.

32 The Hebrew text is a loose paraphrase of Proverbs 23:7.

33 A direct quotation from Job 3:25.

34 The exclamation of the child of the Shunamite when he was suddenly taken ill. Elisha, the prophet, thereafter revives him from his deathly state. II Kings 4:19.

35 Psalms 48:6.

36 The bailiff's charge derives from Deuteronomy 22:27.

37 The Hebrew text is reminiscent of the words of Boaz when he wakes upon the threshing floor to Ruth's presence near him, and is surprised that she does not associate with young men of her own age. Ruth 3:10.

38 A paraphrase of Job 4:14.

39 The bitter water of Numbers 5:22 originally was prescribed as a test for

the infidelity of a woman to her husband. Here Rabbi Amitai uses it to shock Amon in a similar way into confessing that he broke his daughter's betrothal contract with Jedidiah.

40 A loose paraphrase of Isaiah 19:14 and Jeremiah 10:15.

41 The story of Dinah and Shechem is told in Genesis 34.

42 From Habakkuk 3:2—literally, "In wrath, remember compassion."

43 Literally, "Because the way is contrary to me, I am come forth as an adversary." The remark is that of the Lord's Angel to Balaam upon blocking the soothersayer's path. Numbers 22:32.

44 A quotation from Isaiah 5:27 (literally, "without flagging or stumbling").

45 A quotation from I Kings 21:15 (literally, "Arise, take possession of the vineyard [of Naboth]").

46 Greedy, the clever lawyer, rephrases the statement of Ezekiel 37:17 to suit his own purpose. The prophet describes the "sticks" (the tribes of Israel) that shall become "as one [unit]." Greedy, however, construes Ezekiel's "la'ahadim" to mean "*but* one." Both meanings are possible from the Hebrew word.

47 Literally, "necklace-beads," as found in the Song of Songs 4:9. The euphemism is in the same sardonic spirit that moved the frontiersman in the American West to designate the hangman's noose as a "necktie" during the late ninteenth century.

48 Or "a measuring line," as in Zachariah 2:5.

49 Leone is here indulging in delicious word play, for in Hebrew Absalom ("the father of Sholom") is also "Ben-Shlomo"—"the son of Solomon," the latter a variant of the name "Shalom." But in our play the son of Sholom is Jedidiah, so the comparison of the two young men is apt from a linguistic viewpoint.

50 I have here substituted an English pun for that of Leone's Hebrew. In the original text "Absalom . . . was hung upon an oak (ba'eileh), so Jedidiah . . . being hung for these [reasons] (ba'eileh)."

51 A reworking of Ecclesiastes 9:17, "the quiet words of the wise." The Hebrew word "d'varim" may mean both "words" and "legal matters." It is in this latter sense that it becomes the title of the Fifth Book of the Hebrew Scriptures, ordinarily known in its Greek rendering, Deuteronomy.

52 Here Leone makes use of a phrase in Obadiah 14 for poetic effect. Its literal meaning has to do with "standing . . . in the cross-way."

53 The words of Jethro to Moses upon seeing his son-in-law overwhelmed by the number of legal and adminstrative problems that he personally was trying to solve. In Exodus 18:18.

54 Leone shows a weak Amon trying to put the blame for his wrongdoing upon his wife by using the words of Adam, partly in paraphrase, to excuse himself. Genesis 3:13.

55 "The utmost part" is the literal translation, as found in Numbers 23:13.

56 The line is from Psalms 139:6, "Such knowledge is too wonderful for me."
57 A loose rendering of Judges 14:14, "From strength (arrogance), He has brought forth sweetness (modesty)."
58 A loose rendering of Psalm 38:11, "The light of His eyes is gone from me, . . ."
59 Literally the quotation from Job 12:3, "That I did not fall away from you."
60 A direct quotation from Lamentations 5:8, "Slaves rule over (us)."
61 Amitai uses the words of Exodus 19:21, ". . . and many should fall(perish)," to describe Shovel's degradation.
62 An allusion derived from Habakkuk 2:19, where the idol is "(over)laden with gold and silver."
63 Isaiah 41:7. The original reference, however, is not to a marriage, but to a soldering of metal. Here, as well, Leone impishly injects a note of humor into his dialogue.